TRAINING KNOW-HOW
for
CROSS CULTURAL
and
DIVERSITY TRAINERS

by
L. Robert Kohls
with
Herbert L. Brussow

Adult Learning Systems, Inc.
P.O. Box 458
Duncanville, TX 75138-0458

Library of Congress Cataloging-in-Publication Data

Training know-how for cross-cultural and diversity trainers / [edited by] L. Robert Kohls
    with Herbert L. Brussow.
       p. cm.
    Includes bibliographical references and index.
    ISBN 1-887493-04-2
     1. Employees—Training of—Social aspects. 2. Employee training personnel—
    Training of. 3. Cross-cultural orientation. 4. Cross-cultural counseling. I. Kohls, L.
    Robert II. Brussow, Herbert L. (Herbert Leon), 1936- .
    HF5549.5.T7T683   1995
    658.3' 1244--dc20
                                              95-34039
                                                CIP

There is no doubt in my mind that, in this last decade of the 20th century, the intercultural field has become the most important calling to which anyone can respond, for it provides the means of understanding and drawing together the disparate and often antagonistic peoples of our nation and of the world.

L. Robert Kohls

This book is dedicated to the men and women
who carry cross-cultural and diversity training
to the nation and the world.

ACKNOWLEDGEMENTS

Bob Reed, Ph.D., gave freely of his personal time to produce the index and assist in formatting the document and arranging difficult diagrams in a publishable format. Bob's interest in this kind of project is prompted by his deep concern that people who anticipate serving in different cultures be appropriately prepared.

Kirby F. O'Brien's artistic design expertise can be seen in the design of the cover. Kirby took time to read portions of the book in order to conceptualize a design to complement the message of the text.

Throughout the text, acknowledgments are given for copyrighted material on the first page of the text it refers to. Many of the articles included in the text are in the public domain. The authors of such articles are acknowledged where known.

Ted Barnnett, of Basic Computers in La Crescenta, California, freely gave of his time, scanning the original text and running it through an OCR program.

Many individuals shared in the project by proof-reading the text and making other editorial suggestions, for which we express our appreciation.

TABLE OF CONTENTS

FOREWORD

Much of the material in this book was first brought together at the request of the International Society for Intercultural Education, Training and Research (SIETAR International) in a special handbook in 1980. There is even a greater need for the material today because there are so many more cross-cultural and diversity trainers now than there were a decade and a half ago. The numbers of young people who have just discovered the field and who hope to enter it grows larger with each passing year. Yet I continue to be surprised at how many of those who discover cross-cultural training, and who find it to be so glamorous and so exciting, are totally unaware that there is also a related and overlapping field, known as *training*, which they must also master in order to become an effective cross-cultural/diversity trainer. It is for those young people—the lifeblood of the field—that I have revised and reissued *Training Know-How for Cross-Cultural and Diversity Trainers*.

In order to design and deliver the best possible cross-cultural/diversity training, it is necessary to master four separate elements:

- The PHILOSOPHY of the field,
- The TECHNOLOGY of the field,
- The METHODOLOGIES of the field, and
- The PERFORMANCE SKILLS of the trainer.

This book presents, in the shortest format possible, the essentials of all four of these aspects of training.

The **Philosophy of Cross-Cultural Training** forms the base out of which intercultural workshops, training sessions, and courses spring. It is as dependent on educational philosophy (especially the way adults learn) as it is on theories of how different cultural groups can best be brought into meaningful relationships with each other. Pages 15 through 56 of this book concentrate on the philosophy of cross-cultural training, and pages 3 through 11 and pages 59 through 69 are concerned with the philosophy of training in the larger sense.

The **Technology of Cross-Cultural Training** (known as the *Systems Approach to Training* when it was first developed in the mid-1960s) is known today as *Instructional Systems Design* (ISD). Page 71 shows its various parts in list form, and page 72 displays the process diagramatically. Basically, the technology of training refers to the way in which training programs are designed. Its various parts are further discussed on pages 73 through 96.

The **Methodologies of Cross-Cultural Training** refer to the more than 100 kinds of training activities, techniques and strategies—everything from small discussion groups to case studies to role plays, and much more. Pages 118 through 138 introduce you to the full range of training methodologies.

Performance Skills refer to the way in which a trainer actually presents the training to the trainees. This is also called *platform skills* or *stand-up training skills*. These must be achieved through practice before live audiences, with the trainer learning, through actually doing it, to use to maximum advantage all that transpires within the training room (and to keep all potentially distracting influences from having a negative impact on the group). Pages 99 through 115 and 142 are concerned with the performance skills of the trainer.

Training Know-How for Cross-Cultural and Diversity Trainers has been designed so that it can be used in the Training-of-Other-Trainers Workshops or it can be used, equally successfully, by individual trainers who want to improve their understanding and ability in any of the four elements described above.

As you flip through this book, browsing the various articles and lists, you may be surprised to discover the early dates on several of the pieces. This is simply because, as mentioned above, the field of training as we know it today was invented in the mid-1960s, and some of those original contributions are as fresh and applicable today as they were when they were first written.

It is my hope that you will find this book informative and helpful and that it will actually improve your skills as a cross-cultural trainer.

L. Robert Kohls
San Francisco, 1995

TRAINING
AS A RELATIVELY
NEW FORM OF
LEARNING

SECTION TITLES

TRAINING AS A TWENTIETH CENTURY DISCIPLINE
CONTRASTING ROLES OF TRADITIONAL AND EXPERIENTIAL TRAINER
EDUCATION, TRAINING, ORIENTATION AND BRIEFING COMPARED

TRAINING AS A TWENTIETH CENTURY DISCIPLINE

L. Robert Kohls

While learning and education have been with us for a very long time, training is a relatively new activity. It has only been considered a field since about 1965. The activities and approaches which are implied by *training* are not immediately understood by everyone who hears the word. To many people, training is something done to dogs, or something athletes are in, or something which is associated with the toilet habits of small children.

Understood or not, training has sparked a major learning industry, has had broad effects on human resource development in the private sector, and has greatly affected the learning methodologies used in all but the most conservative educational institutions at all levels in America. Significantly, too, training has been associated with cross-cultural learning since training's inception in the mid-1960s.

Training, in order to be understood, must be seen as a field of expertise in and of itself, divorced from the content of any particular training program which you might have in mind. That is to say, a training program always has a specific subject matter which the trainer attempts to transfer to the trainee. But so far as the trainer is concerned, his/her expertise lies not so much in the content being transferred as it does in knowing how to get that content across. Using a subject matter expert to draw information from, an experienced trainer can design and deliver training in a wide variety of topics stretching far beyond his/her own content knowledge of any given field. Training is the master discipline which makes it possible to transfer other disciplines.

Much has been made of the differences between *education* and *training*. I am aware that the distinctions between the two are becoming blurred and that many of the activities formerly associated with training have been borrowed freely by educators during the past decade. This borrowing should be encouraged. As *educational technology* replaces the *teacher training* approach, the two disciplines eventually are likely to merge into one.

To complicate the issue further, many trainers discovered the man who was to become their guru, Malcolm S. Knowles, in the School of Education at Boston University. His book, *The Modern Practice Of Adult Education,* was published in 1970, but it was not generally known to trainers until the mid-1970s.[1] It presents the theoretical and conceptual underpinnings of the field.

The classical and probably still the most definitive comparison of *traditional education* and *training* is that presented by Roger Harrison and Richard L. Hopkins in their 1967 article, "The Design of Cross-Cultural Training: An Alternative to the University Model."[2] Those who want a more complete definition of training and, in particular, how it contrasts with a more traditional academic approach are referred to that article.

Some of the characteristics which distinguish training from traditional classroom education are:

1. An awareness of the different approaches which are most appropriate to the teaching of *content*, those which can best *transfer skills*, and those which can affect *attitudinal* changes. (It is in this latter area that training is often most effective.)

---

[1]Published by Association Press, NY.
[2]*Journal of Applied Behavioral Sciences*, Vol. 3, #4, pp. 431-461.

2. Paying special attention to how adults learn. These findings are based on a large body of research in the behavioral sciences. The main points are:

   - Adults like to be treated like adults

   - They learn most rapidly when they know why they should learn and *buy into* the process

   - They are willing to take responsibility for their own learning

   - They don't like surprises

   - They don't like to be embarrassed (and they don't like potentially embarrassing situations)

   - They like to know where they stand at all times.

   This latter practice has popularized the computer term *feedback* as it is applied to training. To be effective, feedback must be frequent and frank.

3. A strong preference for the experiential approach. *Hands-on* learning and actual practice, whenever appropriate, is used. The inductive approach, where experience precedes *telling*, is preferred. (Many trainers would not even *tell* after the experience but would skillfully pull the responses from their trainees.)

4. The development of a large number of learning methodologies, activities, techniques, *structured experiences* and *instrumented exercises*.[3]

5. Emphasis on *learning how to learn*, which is considered far more valuable than learning a specific body of knowledge.

6. The Systems Approach applied to the development of the training program.[4]

7. Tailoring training to meet the unique needs of individual trainees.

8. Paying special attention to the sequence and mix of training activities.

9. Emphasis given to the *processing* of experiential learning activities. This is usually done in small group discussions (eight or ten is considered an ideal size; never more than twelve) where the trainer helps each trainee express what he or she experienced or learned in the activity just completed. It is not sufficient merely to present one exciting, involving experiential exercise after another without such *processing* to fix the learning in the minds of the trainees.

10. The trainer becomes the central figure in the training program. Trainers need to have a natural charisma and a human concern for the trainees which is immediately apparent to all. They are most generally called *Facilitators*, indicating their role is to facilitate learning, not to pose as learned scholars who present their vast knowledge in eloquent lectures to the trainees. The trainer functions more in the role of *coach* or *guide* than as *leader*. For American cross-cultural training programs, it is essential that trainers have overseas living experience in the target country, and that their attitudes toward the country be positive.

---

[3]Kohls, L. Robert, (1979), *Methodologies for trainers a compendium of learning strategies,* Washington, DC: Future Life Press, lists over 100 such methodologies. William Pfeiffer and John Jones have developed a dozen books of training exercises (six volumes in their *Handbook of Structured Experiences for Human Relations Training* series and nine volumes, to date, in their Annual Handbook for Group Facilitators (1972 to present). These are available from Pfeiffer & Company.

[4]SIETAR has a similar volume, *Intercultural Sourcebook: Cross-Cultural Training Methodologies.* It is available from the Intercultural Press, Yarmouth, Maine.

Contrasting Roles of Traditional and Experiential Trainer

Albert P. Wight

The Experiential Trainer

1. Focuses on the process of learning—learning how to learn.
2. Involves the trainee actively in assuming the responsibility for his/her own learning and change.
3. Helps the trainee learn to be an active information seeker, identifying and making effective use of available resources.
4. Expects the trainee to learn to find and use information as needed to solve problems.
5. Expects the trainee to learn by exploration and discovery, asking questions, formulating and testing hypotheses, solving problems.
6. Focuses on the creative process of identifying and solving open-ended, real-life problems with many possible solutions. There is no expert.
7. Formulates clearly defined objectives based on the identified needs of the trainee.
8. Involves the trainee in the identification of his/her own learning needs and objectives.
9. Involves the trainee in assessment and evaluation of the training experience, information obtained, and progress toward objectives.
10. Avoids giving advice, but helps the trainees explore alternatives and arrive at their own conclusions.
11. Focuses on helping the trainee learn to work effectively with others in cooperative, problem-solving activities.
12. Focuses on group discussions and activities conducted and evaluated by the trainees themselves.

The Traditional Trainer

1. Focuses on teaching of content, facts and information.
2. Assumes the responsibility for deciding what the trainee needs and motivating him/her to learn.
3. Decides what the trainee needs and provides it through lectures reading assignments, films, etc.
4. Expects the trainee to learn the material presented for recall on examinations.
5. Expects the trainee to learn primarily by memorization and formulation of responses to questions asked by the trainer.
6. Focuses on the completion of text-book-type exercises or problems with *one right answer*. The trainer is the expert.
7. Formulates objectives based on covering a specified amount of material.
8. Expects the trainee to accept the objectives specified by the experts for the course.
9. Assesses and evaluates the material he presents, effectiveness of presentation, and performance and progress of each trainee.
10. Assumes the role of the expert, providing expert opinions and advice.
11. Focuses on classroom control; working with others is a distraction, not an objective.
12. Focuses on lectures, group discussions, and other activities led, controlled, and evaluated by the trainer.

The Experiential Trainer

13. Works toward open communication, sharing of ideas and opinions between trainees and the staff, among the staff, and among the trainees.

14. Encourages informality and spontaneity in the training.

15. Promotes a questioning attitude, challenging of expert opinion, reliance on the trainee's own judgment.

16. Invites ideas. suggestions, and criticism from the trainees.

17. Involves the trainees in decision-making regarding training activities. Assumes that objectives might be clarified or new objectives identified that will modify the content and activities of the training.

18. Uses the training as a laboratory, capitalizing on learning opportunities presented by unplanned incidents and problems encountered in the training.

The Traditional Trainer

13. Focuses on one-way communication from the trainer to the trainees with little communication from the trainees, among the trainees, or even among staff.

14. Establishes formal procedures and control in the classroom.

15. Promotes respect for the trainer as an expert, distrust of the trainee's own judgment.

16. Discourages suggestions or criticism from the trainees.

17. Makes the decisions or carries out decisions made by the staff. Considers that a well-planned training program will not need to be modified.

18. Attempts to prevent disruption of the planned activities and schedule, either ignoring incidents or problems or dealing with them as quickly as possible.

CRITERIA FOR EXPERIENTIAL TRAINING/LEARNING

Albert P. Wight

The following criteria can be used in planning, designing, or evaluating an experiential training program. Criteria that relate to traditional as much as to experiential programs are not included. These are criteria that distinguish an experiential program from a traditional program. The more the program meets these criteria, the more experiential it is,

1. Does the program involve participants in their own learning agenda (personal ownership and responsibility) as opposed to someone else's (i.e., the trainer's, textbook's, or organization's)?

2. Does the program help participants identity and clarify needs, objectives, and priorities (knowledge, understanding, attitudes, behavior, skills) as opposed to providing all of the objectives?

3. Does the program engage each participant at a personal, meaningful level in activities that focus on learning through experience and discovery as opposed to didactic instruction and learning through listening, reading, and memorization?

4. Do the activities/problems/tasks have face validity—that is, are they readily perceived as relevant, important, meaningful given the role and responsibilities for which participants are preparing?

5. If participants' lack of experience does not allow them to see the relevance, are they confronted with situations/experiences/problems that help them see it?

6. Do the activities confront participants with:
   - questions they have difficulty answering
   - problems they have difficulty solving
   - situations they have difficulty understanding
   - dilemmas they have difficulty resolving
   - decisions they have to make
   - consequences they need to examine
   - reactions they don't anticipate
   - differences of opinion they need to resolve
   - situations that might be difficult to handle?

7. Do the activities generate data from the participants themselves (beliefs, attitudes, opinions, behavior, etc.) as opposed to hypothetical data or data from other groups (i.e., experts, experiments, research, war stories)?

8. Does the program require participants to do their own thinking as opposed to learning what the trainer or experts think?

9. Does the program elicit responses based on the participants own perceptions, understanding, ideas, opinions, theories, as opposed to requiring memorization or guessing of the *correct* response or trainer's/expert's preference?

10. Does the program promote group discussion—sharing of ideas, beliefs, attitudes, opinions, perceptions, evaluations?

11. Does the program require the participants to examine and test their own attitudes, beliefs, theories, and behaviors against those of others and the reality they can expect to encounter?

12. Does the program provide feedback to the participants?

13. Is the focus on self-evaluation as opposed to trainer or expert evaluation of participants?

14. Does the program promote participant evaluation and decisions regarding personal use and application of learnings?

15. Does the program provide resources/opportunities to participants to obtain information they feel or come to recognize they need?

16. Does the program provide training and practice in real-life problem-solving and decision-making in interaction with other persons?

17. Does the program provide opportunities for skill practice?

18. Does the program promote independence, initiative, resourcefulness, and self-confidence as opposed to dependence on the trainer, experts, and procedures?

19. Does the program help participants "learn how to learn" on their own through their experience following training?

20. Is the focus in the program on process—emergent needs, goals, and design—as opposed to religiously following predetermined objectives, content, and schedule?

EDUCATION, TRAINING, ORIENTATION AND BRIEFING COMPARED

L. Robert Kohls

Learning Mode	Education	Training	Orientation	Briefing
Major Application	Presents large bodies of content knowledge and is often used to develop in-depth mastery of one or more subjects.	Focuses on *process* and/or developing competency in performing specific skills, or meeting specified objectives in a cost effective manner.	Prepares a person to understand and function effectively in a new or radically different environment and achieves this shift in the least traumatic manner.	Provides a broad overview or can focus on a particular part of a large program in the most time effective way.
Overall Purpose	The full development of the mind's capabilities, as well as the imparting or acquiring of knowledge—sometimes for no other purpose than for the sheer joy of learning.	To provide practical, results-oriented learning. This aim has often been applied to a professional, vocational or military context. Aimed at achieving predetermined and clearly stated objectives which are then measured to determine whether they have been met.	To orient a person to a place or position, especially to new situations, environments, ideas, values, or operating principles. Helps a person understand how to operate comfortably in an unfamiliar setting.	To provide the background of an organization, topic, place or situation in a concise and focused manner.

Source: From L. Robert Kohls. (1987). "Four Traditional Approaches to Developing Cross-Cultural Preparedness in Adults: Education, Training, Orientation and Briefing." *International Journal of Intercultural Relations.* Volume 11, pages 89-106. (Included on pages 31 to 42 of this book).

Learning Mode	Education	Training	Orientation	Briefing
Methodologies	Through the teacher, often serving as a role model who passes on knowledge (or a particular specialization or approach) to the student. Lecture-presentations are the most common methodology; also question and answer sessions, reading assignments, written assignments, and periodic examinations.	Experiential and participant-centered exercises; emphasizing hands-on experience, practice and drills. Training has access to an extensive repertoire of highly developed methodologies to accomplish a variety of clearly designated ends.	Helps participants shift from their old orientation to a new one by *starting where they are* at point of entry and introducing them to approaches which are more appropriate to the new environment. Draws on methodologies borrowed from training and education.	Systematically presents cogent, highly organized, simplified and sequenced information, often in chart form. Usually followed by question-and-answer session to clear up ambiguous points.
Time Required	Longest-term of all the modes. Now popularly considered a life-long activity (yet formal education is generally thought of as completed upon receipt of an undergraduate university degree). Frequently divided into segments (such as courses, class periods, semesters, grade levels or years).	Programs vary greatly in duration. Most commonly last one day to two weeks. However, a sequenced training schedule with a number of separate training courses can last from three to six months.	Usually from one-half day to one week in length.	Shortest-term of all the modes: as short as ten or fifteen minutes and as long as an hour or an hour and a half.

Learning Mode	Education	Training	Orientation	Briefing
Delivered by	Educators, Teachers, Professors, Teaching Fellows, all often with advanced degrees.	Trainers or *Facilitators*; also by the Trainees themselves. Uses Subject Matter Experts in the development of the program (but rarely in its delivery).	Has not developed generic names to describe the person who delivers. Often uses a functional title such as *Program Coordinator* or *Session Leader*.	Experts (who usually are incumbents in in-house positions).
Strongest Features	Most thorough in its coverage (since time is often not a major factor). Generally used in delivering large bodies of content information. Especially effective in the theoretical realm and in focusing, in-depth, on a specialized field (but most passive and boring since there is little active participation).	Most active and *involving*. Most cost-effective. Often has an evaluation component designed into it to determine whether learning objectives were met. Trainees contribute to their own learning, thus gaining content information, skill in applying and self confidence.	Most supportive since it does not remove participants from original orientation framework until new one is firmly established. Transforms while minimizing the shock of the foreign environment.	Most time effective mode. Achieves maximum amount of information transfer in shortest possible time. Spotlights most relevant and essential information so recipient is not required to sort out the essential from the non-essential.
Examples of Appropriate Intercultural Content	Area Studies material (historical, political, economic, social, aesthetic, etc.); Language acquisition (which accompanies cross-cultural training).	Cultural Awareness; Specific Skills (precisely specified by carefully stated behavioral objectives).	Practical Information concerning survival skills (e.g. using bus or subway, finding an apartment, shopping, etc.) Customs, with emphasis on differences; Institutions, and Values and Comparative Values.	Broad Overview of the field; Relevant Background Information that should be taken into account; Description of Current Situation.

INTERCULTURAL
TRAINING
SPECIFICALLY

Section Titles

Intercultural Training for Overseas Posting

Four Traditional Approaches to Developing Cross-Cultural Preparedness in Adults: Education, Training, Orientation and Briefing

Kinds of Intercultural Training Available

What Intercultural Training Will Do

Content and Sequencing of Cross-Cultural Training

Seven Issues in Cross-Cultural Training

Carrying American-Designed Training Overseas

INTERCULTURAL TRAINING FOR OVERSEAS POSTING

L. Robert Kohls

The formation of the multinational/global corporation, the economic recession of the 1990s, and the search for foreign markets have caused many major American companies to realize that it is a very costly mistake to send the wrong employee to represent an organization overseas. Even the right representative needs careful preparation to be maximally productive. Simply because an executive has had a successful career in the United States does not mean that person will automatically be equally successful in an alien and sometimes hostile environment.

It is estimated that it costs an average of $150,000 to $250,000 in direct costs for an American company to bring a mid-level executive home early from a foreign assignment. There is no way to estimate how much additional damage, in terms of lost business and ruined company reputation, such a mistake may have caused before the person was finally evacuated. Families have literally broken up and careers have been ruined from such a potentially traumatic experience. It is sheer suicide not to select the best possible candidates for overseas service and then not to give them the best possible pre-departure training and the best home office and field support available.

On the positive side, such training will not only prevent calamities, it can also be expected to boost productivity, help an American manager motivate foreign national employees, and generally make such a person more effective in a foreign environment.

American senior and mid-level executives can, in one week's time or less, be prepared to interact effectively with those whose language, culture, customs, business practices, and basic values are radically different from our own. They can even learn to enjoy the foreign environment, which might, if they were unaided, seem too threatening or too unappealing.

Foreign-born personnel coming to work at the company's American headquarters will also require similar intercultural training in order to facilitate their adaptation to life in this country.

In short, all personnel who are not already bicultural (by birth and early enculturation) in the culture of the country to which they have been assigned need intercultural training. The overseas living experience should be a positive, exhilarating growth experience. That will not just happen if left to chance. Without pre-departure training, only from 15 to 20 percent of your company's *successful* American mid-level executives can be expected to function fairly effectively in the overseas environment. Without intercultural training, as many as 40 to 60 percent will fail—either necessitating early removal or staying on but functioning far below their normal U.S. productivity level. With effective intercultural training, the failure rate can be reduced to 5 percent or less. With such training, even the 15 to 20 percent who would have succeeded without training will be able to produce at a far higher level. This makes intercultural training essential and cost-effective for all personnel assigned overseas.

The results of intercultural training will be fewer early returnees, lower relocation costs, higher job performance, and greater productivity. You cannot afford *not* to offer intercultural training for all your personnel assigned abroad.

Definition of Intercultural Training

Intercultural training is training that gives people the necessary information, skills, and attitudes to enable them to adjust to and function productively in a country other than their own. Intercultural training grows out of a multi-disciplinary effort. The academic disciplines of intercultural communication (now taught at more than 200 universities in the United States), cross-cultural psychology, international management, communication, the social and behavioral sciences, and cultural anthropology have, along with area studies, provided the necessary theory and content knowledge for intercultural training. The pedagogical approaches that have developed around adult learning theories and concepts have furnished the training methodology.

The above mentioned content areas are combined, generally, to create a one or two week, country-specific training program. The one week version, because it obviously requires only about half the cost and half the time away from the job, is by far the most popular among corporate clients. The one week schedule must, of course, be tightly packed, utilizing most of the evening hours as well, and it usually does not allow time to include any language training (which must then be undertaken entirely in-country).

Although it is too ambitious an aim to actually achieve in two or three years (the length of the average overseas assignment), it is still worthwhile to consider the desirable end of any overseas living experience to be the creation of a being who is *bicultural*, who acts according to the value orientation, customs, and expectations of his or her home country when that is appropriate and according to those of the host country when that is appropriate. It is possible (although difficult) to achieve and it is worth whatever trouble it takes to learn to see the world from another person's perspective. Once this is achieved, such an employee will be far more valuable even back at the American office.

It is not recommended to design an intercultural training program of less than three days; yet many independent trainers and many institutions, when pressed to do so will develop a one or two day program. Any amount of training is better than none, of course, but one should not expect such short programs to achieve anything more than a basic and very incomplete awareness that living overseas will be quite different from living in the States. It hardly gives time to allay the natural fears involved with such a move and to give a realistic understanding of what the in-country experience will be like. More questions will be raised than answered by too short a course.

All personnel who are assigned overseas for six months or more should be given a solidly packed program of from three days' to one week's duration. This includes spouses and all teenage children who will accompany their parents overseas. Recent studies indicate that in four out of five early returning families, it was the spouse who experienced the major adjustment difficulties and was the cause of early return. (This, of course, is not due to any inherent weakness of spouses but, rather, to the fact that spouses often have more unprogrammed time, and they are often forced to interact more with the marketplace of the host country.)

In addition, all the stateside personnel who will provide home office support services should be enrolled in such courses. If these personnel are added, a few at a time, to courses scheduled for transferring employees, this can usually be accomplished without raising the costs of training very much. This is particularly true if the institution offering the training realizes that such a service is likely to produce increased future business. (The suggested content for the initial one week pre-departure training program is detailed in a later section, entitled *Content/Coverage.*)

Almost as essential as the pre-departure course we have been describing is an *in-country relocation assistance program*, in which experienced overseas personnel— Americans who are well adjusted to the host country and very familiar with how to get things done within that culture, as well as with the feelings and needs of newly expatriated Americans—are there to help the newly arrived, disoriented, and frightened family settle in. They can and do help the family feel "at home" and assist in whatever specific ways may be needed. This may mean finding adequate housing at the right price, arranging for utilities hookups, completing the required residence and work documents, selecting schools and enrolling the children in them, finding a language tutor, recommending family doctors and dentists, opening a checking account, and the hundreds of other things that seem so difficult to arrange in a new country and in an "impossible" language. For all the help they give during those first traumatic days and weeks, such services[1] are very reasonably priced and highly recommended. It is very comforting to know that assistance is only a phone call away. This service helps ensure that the newcomers will get off to a good start.

Also not to be overlooked is the eventual need for a short (perhaps two or three day) program to prepare the employee psychologically to return to America as the overseas tour draws to a close. This reentry training program is particularly indicated when the employee has performed well overseas. A good rule of thumb is that the person who has adjusted quickly and well to the overseas environment can be expected to experience the greatest difficulty in readjusting to his or her own country. Many Americans—invariably those with the highest overseas performance record—report that the return culture shock they experience is far greater than the initial culture shock in adjusting to the foreign country.

Objectives of Intercultural Training

The objectives of a one week intercultural training program should be to:

1. Prepare Americans without previous overseas living experience (of at least one continuous year) to adjust positively to living in a foreign environment.

2. Make these Americans aware of their own previous socialization as Americans— specifically, what their American values are, how unique and unusual those values are in a world context, and how *strange* Americans sometimes seem to people of other cultures.

3. Introduce these Americans to the logic of the foreign culture to which they are going and give as complete and accurate a picture of that culture as is possible in the limited time available.

4. Ease these Americans through the inevitable experience of "culture shock."[2]

---

[1]Bennett & Associates, 135 Ashland Avenue, Wilmette, IL 60091; Prudential Relocation Intercultural Services, 2555 55th Street, Boulder, CO 80301; and International Orientation Resources, 500 Skokie Boulevard, Suite 600, Northbrook, Illinois 60062, are the leading providers of in-country relocation assistance.
[2]For a description of this phenomenon and for helpful suggestions on how to move through it, see Chapters 18 and 19 of L. Robert Kohls, *Survival kit for overseas living,* Yarmouth, ME: Intercultural Press, 1995.

5. Facilitate a rapid and positive adjustment of each family member to the host culture, enable the employee to work productively in the host culture, and lead eventually to the successful completion of the full tour of assignment.

A two week program could be expected to achieve these same five objectives, plus expand on the amount of information covered by objective 3. In addition, it should include from twenty to forty hours of language training. A one or two day program could be expected to accomplish little more than objectives 1, 2, and 3.

Essential Conditions for Intercultural Training

This section addresses the questions of when and where the training should be done.

It is recommended that the training be conducted off-site, away from the pressures and distractions of the office and physically removed from the worries and cares of making a major move. It is also recommended that the living accommodations and training facilities be as physically comfortable, well equipped, and conducive to learning as possible.

When the training should be presented, in relation to the move, is not such an easy question to answer. There are some advantages to having it further from the move and other advantages to placing it nearer to the actual transfer. In no case should it be given more than two months or less than two weeks prior to the move.

The advantage of scheduling it two months before relocation is that the employees will be able to take a more objective, detached, and reflective approach to learning about the country. They will be able to put the assignment and the cultural comparisons into perspective, without having their minds occupied with the thousand and one decisions that have to be made before the move. Full attention can be given to the questions and concerns raised by the training itself. There is a danger, on the other hand, that the employee will be too detached and that the issues raised by the training will be over-intellectualized and received at too high a level of abstraction. Any language included in the training program may be largely forgotten by the time it is needed. This is the right amount of time, however, to thoughtfully and objectively consider if you need to change a will or prepare one, whether to sell the house or rent it, and what to do about the children's schooling.

When the training is given one or two weeks before boarding the airplane, the participants tend to be in too stressed a state to get the most out of it. They are too concerned with packing and deciding what to take and what to place in storage to give themselves fully to the issues raised in the training program. At the same time, though, the move is near enough to be very real and they are fully motivated to learn all they can about the pros and cons of their new environment. What they learn—particularly any language study—will be reinforced in-country while it is still fresh.

There is some evidence that those who receive the training program two months or more before entering the country tend to relate less to host nationals when they finally arrive, preferring to spend all their free time with other Americans. In other words, the intellectual and detached approach fostered by their attitude toward the training seems to carry over to the field.

If those who are scheduled to receive their training two or three weeks before their flight could have all the details of their move taken care of before the training begins, this shorter lead time clearly provides the optimal motivation and results. This presupposes, of course, that the parent company has a long-range planning cycle (so that last minute assignments are not made) and a supportive personnel system to offer counsel and advice that will help the employee make the difficult decisions and not put them off until the last minute.

The Trainer's Role and Functions

To undertake training in the intercultural area, the trainer must have all the following qualifications:

1. Area knowledge of the target country, gained either through first-hand experience or through study.

2. Living experience in the target country (a minimum of two years and preferably longer).

3. A positive attitude toward the country and its people.

4. The experience of having lived through culture shock.

5. A fundamental knowledge of basic American values and implicit cultural assumptions and how to articulate them.

6. Experience as a trainer—especially as a stand-up trainer—and particularly in processing a variety of experiential learning techniques.

7. Interest in training for content as well as process.

Availability of Intercultural Training

Many private institutions and scores of independent trainers across the country have the experience and country expertise necessary to design and deliver cost-effective intercultural training for your personnel. It is a matter of finding the right trainers and helping them tailor a program that meets your specific needs. There are disadvantages to using independent consultants for this type of training. Individually they may be very good, but even the best cannot be familiar with all the countries to which a corporation may wish to send its personnel. Of course, they can bring in additional trainers to provide such country expertise, but their resources are severely limited, especially when compared to the larger companies that specialize in intercultural training. The Business Council for International Understanding (BCIU), by contrast, is able to include as many as fifteen different experts in a one week program. It is difficult for an independent trainer even to identify such a roster, much less to finance the operation until payment is eventually received from the client. This argues in favor of patronizing the well-established training firm with proven results and satisfied clients, but the corporation should not overlook the availability of excellent cross-cultural trainers in its own community.

Two organizations that might be helpful in recommending members in your city or region who could provide cross-cultural training are:

- SIETAR International (the Society for Intercultural Education, Training and Research), 808 17th Street, NW, Suite 200, Washington, D.C. 20006 (the leading professional organization in the field). Contact Mr. David Santini at (202) 446-7883.

- The local chapter of ASTD (American Society for Training and Development), whose national headquarters is at 1640 King Street, Alexandria, Virginia 22313, (703) 683-8100. The local ASTD chapter, if there is one in your area, should be listed in your telephone directory.

There are several reputable institutions with a proven track record in delivering inter-cultural training:

- The Business Council for International Understanding (BCIU), Suite 244, Foxhall Square, 3301 New Mexico Avenue, NW, Washington, D.C. 20016, is the grandparent of such organizations, regularly serving many of the Fortune 500 companies for the past thirty-five years. It most often develops a one week program without language or a two week program with forty hours of language training included. It can pull together a quality program with very little lead time because of its large roster of country experts who lecture on a broad range of country-specific topics. BCIU is based at the American University. Contact Mr. Gary Lloyd at (202) 686-2771.

- Prudential Relocation Intercultural Services (PRIS) (formerly Moran, Stahl and Boyer (MS&B)), 2555 55th Street, Boulder, Colorado 80301, is another pioneer in providing cross-cultural training for the overseas assignment as well as in-country relocation assistance. In addition, PRIS provides complete services to manage the physical move of individuals or of entire companies anywhere in the world and a selection service to ensure that the right people are chosen for overseas service.

  PRIS's approach to intercultural training is more experiential than most. This is combined with solid country-specific information, under the coordination of a master trainer. In addition to designing a five or six day training program (with from sixteen to twenty-two hours of language training), PRIS schedules open-enrollment courses for several key countries. Contact Mr. Gary Wederspahn at (303) 449-8440.

- Clarke Consulting Group (CCG), 3 Lagoon Drive, Suite 230, Redwood City, California 94065, has had considerable success in providing long-term, two-way training for major American and Japanese companies engaged in joint ventures. It has also developed programs for Japanese high-level managers managing plants in this country that are staffed with American employees. For large numbers of immigrant laborers working in American factories, CCG has designed programs to introduce them both to the United States and to the culture of the large corporation. Pre-departure training is also custom designed on request. Contact Dr. Clifford Clarke at (415) 591-8100.

- Bennett & Associates (B&A), One North Franklin Suite 750, Chicago, Illinois 60606, is a full-service company able to meet almost all intercultural training and consulting needs: preparation of Americans and third-country nationals for overseas assignment, international management consulting, multicultural team building, joint venture preparation of both parties, and one of the best repatriation programs to help the returning expatriate move back into the home-based assignment. B&A also has overseas representatives in twenty countries, and it can provide initial settling-in assistance in more than eighty-five cities worldwide. Contact Ms. Rita Bennett at (312) 251-9000.

- International Orientation Resources (IOR), 500 Skokie Boulevard, Suite 600, Northbrook, Illinois 60062, is a full-service cross-cultural training provider for multinational corporations. IOR's capabilities include candidate selection and assessment, predeparture training for international assignment, on-the-spot destination assistance for personnel newly assigned to over 100 cities worldwide, language training and repatriation training, in addition to global management training tailored to a specific multiethnic group's needs, as well as consulting services which are also designed to meet a particular situation. Contact Ms. Noel A. Kreicker at (708) 205-0066.

- Global Vision Group (GVG), 484 Lake Park Avenue, Suite 11, Oakland, California 94610, provides a full-service consultation, training, and OD system to assist a corporation to *go international* or to *go global* (i.e. to increase and modernize its international operations). Everything from the initial conceptualization, organization and planning, all the way through to market research and delivery of the internationally appropriate product anywhere in the world are part of GVG's total capability. This includes, of course, all fourteen of the categories discussed elsewhere in this chapter under the heading *The Range of Intercultural Training Programs Available*. Contact Mr. Claude Schnier at (510) 834-6135.

- The East West Group (EWG), 80 Rancho Dr., Mill Valley, California 94941, is a full-service firm of specialized consultants and trainers of the highest calibre in the United States, Japan, China, all countries in the Pacific Rim, Europe and Latin America. EWG is affiliated with content and process experts in more than 60 countries worldwide. Specialties include developing global operations, leadership team-building in multicultural environments, managing international projects and project teams, and establishing international partnerships and alliances, joint ventures, etc. Contact Mr. Dean Engel at (415) 383-3375.

- Renwick & Associates (R&A), Suite 4, 7333 East Monterey Way, Scottsdale, Arizona 85251, in addition to providing the full range of intercultural training, specializes in preliminary site surveys for companies about to relocate overseas. R&A also consults with companies regarding personnel screening and selection and the evaluation of overseas performance. Its pre-departure programs for Americans assigned abroad usually run from three to five days, as do its orientation programs for foreign nationals coming to the United States. R&A's programs are experientially based, and they are tailored to the customer's needs. Designing simulations and developing audio-visual materials are among its capabilities. Contact Mr. George Renwick at (602) 949-0130.

- Global Dynamics, 19 Wilkinson Road, Randolph, New Jersey 07869, can design and present briefing programs to help your company do business (or increase your business) in any country or region of the world. In addition, they offer intercultural training seminars, globalization audits, as well as workshops on international team building, international joint venture management, international marketing analysis, international negotiation skills, and programs to help your company increase its sales in European, Latin American, and Asian markets. Contact Dr. Neil Goodman at (201) 927-9135.

- Transcultural Services, 712 NW Westover Terrace, Portland, Oregon 97210, can provide two to five day or two week pre-departure training, training for foreign nationals coming to the United States, and training for American managers of large numbers of refugees in a company's work force. Transcultural's pre-departure training places special emphasis on developing effective cross-cultural communication skills and on helping the spouse to manage in the foreign setting. It can also provide full relocation services, including arranging schooling for dependents when the placement is in an isolated area. Contact Ms. Nessa Lowenthal at (503) 497-1066.

- Moran Associates, 5000 North Wilkinson Road, Paradise Valley, Arizona 85253, can provide intercultural training anywhere in the United States. This includes two to five day courses for employees and their families bound for overseas, as well as two to five day courses for foreign managers relocating in the United States. In addition,

Moran Associates often works with American managers going on selected assignments for short periods of time (rather than for extended overseas assignments). This
program develops such skills as problem solving, conflict resolution, and contract
negotiation in the foreign context. Contact Dr. Robert Moran at (602) 946-8042.

- Karani Lam and Associates: Managing Across Cultures (KLA), 12 Chesterford
  Road, Winchester, Massachusetts 01890, is a cross-cultural management consulting
  and training firm with associates in many European, Asian and Latin American
  countries. KLA offers support to transnational and domestically diverse corporations
  and international organizations functioning across cultures. KLA assists organizations in all fourteen categories of training listed elsewhere in this article with special
  strengths in international team building for multinational joint ventures, and particularly for doing business with India. Contact Dr. Zareen Karani Lam de Araoz at
  Phone: (617) 721-7546 or Fax: (617) 721-7543.

- Intercultural Communication, Inc., P.O. Box 14358, University Station, Minneapo-
  lis, Minnesota 55414, offers two or three day briefings and one week pre-departure
  programs for Americans newly assigned overseas. It also presents a special program,
  Introduction to Life in the United States, for foreign nationals coming to America.
  Contact Ms. Helen McNulty at (612) 545-4180.

- W. Shabaz Associates (WSA), 5255 North Lakeshore Drive, Holland, Michigan
  49424, provides pre-departure training for people bound for any country in the world
  and a lot more: training for foreign nationals coming into the United States, reentry
  training for people returning to their countries of origin, intercultural training for
  Americans who, increasingly, need to interface with the rest of the world, and for
  Americans working with a culturally diverse work force here at home. They are
  willing to take their training programs anywhere. Contact Mr. Wayne Shabaz at
  (616) 786-4500.

- The Washington International Center, Meridian House International, 1630 Crescent
  Place, NW, Washington, D.C. 20009, specializes in helping foreign nationals understand and adjust to living in the United States. Each year they train nationals from
  more than 140 countries, and have been doing so since 1950. Their standard course
  is one week long, with extended training available if desired. In addition to Washington, they also offer their training regularly in Seattle and Miami. Contact Ms. Carole
  Watt at (202) 332-1025.

The Range of Intercultural Training Programs Available

Although the primary focus of this chapter is training to prepare Americans for overseas assignments, most intercultural trainers are able to deliver several kinds of training
and consultation of value to the corporate sector operating in an increasingly internationally oriented environment. The training programs they can offer are relevant both to
multinational or global business ventures as well as to managing ethnic diversity in the
domestic workplace. Whether dealing with the world at large or the world at home, both
applications are really only two sides of the same intercultural coin.

The workshops and interventions listed below illustrate the wide range of intercultural offerings currently available:

1. *Relocation training* (also referred to as *pre-departure training* or *country-specific
   training*) is the type that is the main subject of this chapter. Its purpose is to prepare
   a person who has been assigned to work in a foreign country to understand how that
   country, its people and their norms and expectations are different from those of his

or her own country. Of course, the coverage would differ widely for each country; particularly so, depending on whether this is the executive's first or fifth foreign assignment. In other words, the training must be tailored to the needs of the individual or group being assigned overseas.

2. *Initial on-site support* (also known as *in-country support* or *settling-in support*) provides the additional assurances, specific recommendations, contacts and answers to a multitude of unanswered questions for the newly arrived manager and his or her family. It should be made available on retainer for the first three or four months of the foreign sojourn. This sort of consultation could, of course, be provided by a company staff member or spouse who has been in-country for a year or more, but for good reason it is generally recommended that this person not have company connections, because of the fact that he or she may, as part of the required duty, have to nurse the family members through their worst period of culture shock when, emotionally, they will not be at their best; and it will not help if the employees have to worry about any of this information ever finding its way into personnel files or even into the company's corridor gossip channels.

3. *Reentry training and repatriation counseling* help the employee and his or her family readjust to life back in the home country after the foreign assignment has been completed. The need for this training is mentioned elsewhere in the chapter, but it is seldom seen as a real need by those who decide who should receive what training back at headquarters. Yet *reverse culture shock* is a painful reality, oddly enough, particularly for those who did the best job of adjusting overseas. They really do need all the help they can get in fitting in and getting *up to speed* back in the home office. It is a far more difficult task than anyone who has never had the experience can realize.

4. *Managing diversity in the domestic work force*—for mid-level managers—has been one of the fastest growing training programs to develop in the past few years. This demand has been triggered by the rapid rise in the entry of ethnic groups, women, homosexuals and physically disadvantaged people into the U.S. work force. The white, male, middle-class managers who were always so successful, in the past, at managing the largely white, male, middle-class entrants into the work-force have suddenly discovered, to their horror, that what used to work is now proving to be absolutely ineffective or, worse yet, actually counterproductive with the new diverse work force they are expected to be able to manage—and they realize they need help to learn how to motivate and manage this new work force.

5. *Supervisory skills for diverse domestic employees* is a training program that is needed just as urgently on the supervisory level, and for the same reason. Front-line supervisors cannot afford to waste another day before they master the skills that are successful in getting their diverse work-force members to work together cooperatively and productively.

6. *Multinational team building*—on all levels—is more of an OD intervention than a training activity, and it is indicated whenever you have two or more nationalities and/or *ethnic* groups who must work together cooperatively and productively on a single project. It requires an honest effort, led by a skilled group facilitator who can help each component culture understand how they are similar to and different from all the other cultural groups involved as well as acknowledge where and how each group will have to give a little for the group to work together harmoniously and effectively.

Such an intervention can be equally successful within a multi-ethnic group that is just newly being formed or within one which has been together for some time but which definitely needs help to be able to function more effectively.

7. *Intercultural awareness training* is obviously indicated for the person about to leave for an international posting, but it is equally essential for the home-based mid-level and upper-level management personnel (and even for the board members) of companies who are about to *go international* or who intend to step up their global activities.

    The international arena requires a new level of awareness, a new way of looking at the world and your company's role in it. Although each culture has formed each national group in a particular way (it has turned Americans into Americans at the same time that Chinese were being turned into Chinese, and so on), it has also tricked us into believing that our way is not merely our way but that it should be the universal way. This is not only patently untrue, worse yet, it can be disastrous to move into the international arena with this superior attitude in our heads. Intercultural awareness training will put you into the right frame of mind to make your international venture a success, and it should be given, from top to bottom, to all the home office staff who will have anything whatsoever to do with your company's international operation.

8. *Intercultural communication skills* is a course for managers who need to communicate face-to-face or phone-to-phone with people from other countries. These may be foreigners working under their direction here in America, or the American managers may well be in positions that require their ability to communicate with various ethnic groups in the domestic work force. Or they may need to make frequent overseas flights to a variety of countries. Such a workshop as this will develop the skills that are most effective in communicating with foreign nationals whose English may be limited, or highly accented and out of recent practice.

9. *Management training within international organizations*, such as, for example, any of the United Nations organizations or the World Bank—where people from multiple countries need to work together, at a very high level, to accomplish common international goals—can be helpful. This is, in effect, *management skills development*, but the task is made enormously more difficult because each manager is coming to the assignment with vastly different expectations, created by his or her own enculturation, which has caused him or her to view *management* with widely differing interpretations. All these conflicting definitions and expectations need to be brought out into the open and thoroughly discussed and, under the skilled hands of an intercultural facilitator, the groups needs to be brought to a consensus agreement as to which management concept and approach they can agree to use within their working group.

10. *Joint venture preparation* is made to order for the American company about to enter a joint venture agreement with a foreign company. The intercultural trainer works with a team from each of the companies, preparing the team to expect and adjust to the cultural and business practices of the other team; then the intercultural trainer will also join in the negotiation process and he or she will remain on retainer throughout the first full year of operation, facilitating both sides in understanding where the other side is coming from and why. This mutual intervention has proved to be extremely successful in getting the effort off to a profitable start.

11. *International human resources management* personnel often need many of the services and areas of expertise an intercultural trainer can provide. These services cover a broad range of training programs: compensation packages and practices; the realities of overseas living (either in a generic way or focused on a specific country); the acculturation cycle which people go through in the process of adjusting to a foreign country; and helping the company's returning employees through the difficult reentry process.

12. *Americanization training for foreign nationals* working with American-owned subsidiaries and/or American based companies, as well as those foreign students who have decided to study at American universities, can be of significant benefit. This training can be either a brief workshop or a semester-long course to prepare the foreign nationals to function appropriately within the radically different work or study expectations they will encounter in this country (even if they are coming from a western European country).

13. *International negotiation facilitation* is provided by some intercultural trainers. They offer both generic and country-specific preparation in conducting negotiations on an international level. They can also be employed to act as neutral mediators who actually conduct the negotiation, accompanied by the management representatives from your company, if you wish to use their services to facilitate the process.

14. *Protocol to receive international representatives* is another area for training. If your company does not have a director of protocol, you would be well advised to call in an intercultural consultant to be briefed on the arrangements necessary to receive whatever level of visiting dignitary you are expecting to host. More than one American company has done irreparable damage by failing to treat visiting officials with the courtesies they normally receive (and therefore have come to expect).

Key Concepts and Principles

Intercultural training should be built on the following basic concepts:

1. There would be no need to train people to function in other cultures if there were no such thing as ethnocentrism. It is our ethnocentrism—and all people are equally ethnocentric—that makes us think our own culture is superior and all others are inferior, that our ways of doing things are inherently better than anyone else's. If there were no ethnocentrism, we would have no trouble considering various cultures as having discovered different but equally valid solutions to the problems of life.

   Although we usually think of ethnocentrism as a negative force, it also serves a positive end. Ethnocentrism is the major influence in society that preserves the different cultures and gives groups (particularly minority groups) pride in their own identity. In fact, ethnocentrism gives every person his or her first identity—a sense of similarity to and identification with the group into which he or she has been born.

   Yet it is this strong and magnetic force that must be reduced if we are to make the essential point with which all intercultural training begins: *Although you are personally happy to have been born in your own country and into your own ethnic group, and although you feel very strongly that, for you, your own ways are the best, yet you must realize that other people feel just as strongly about their own cultures as you do about yours. For **them, their** cultures are the best. In this sense, one culture is not **better** than any other—only different from all the rest.* Simple though it sounds, this is not an easy message to get across.

The second point follows easily: *Given that cultures have devised different sets of solutions, and given that some of those solutions are very different from your own, and given that you have been assigned and are going to one of those different cultures, you had better start learning as much as you can about that culture.*

2. The desired result of intercultural training is to produce a person who is *bicultural*— that is, who can function in either of two cultures when it is appropriate to do so. Its purpose is not to train the employee to stop being an American, for example, and, transform him or her into a Japanese, or whatever else. No one is asking employees to give up their citizenship or their personal value system, nor are they expected to do something that goes beyond their own sense of morality. But where their ethics are not violated, it makes sense to function, while in another culture, according to the customs and ways of operating that will be effective in that culture, does it not?

3. When people first encounter another culture, they cannot help but notice its isolated parts. Some will seem surprisingly similar to their own way of doing things; some will be alarmingly different. And when they notice these differences, they will be tempted to compare them, out of context, with the corresponding aspects of their own culture. This is counterproductive and unfair to the other culture. What they should do, instead, is try to learn how that particular phenomenon fits into all the other related aspects of that culture. As they learn more of these interrelationships, they will soon discover the *logic* of that culture, and they will begin to see that *everything* in that culture (just as everything in their own culture) is interdependent and interrelated. They should actively seek to discover the totality of that new culture in all its complex and multifarious facets. That exercise could be fascinating enough to keep them occupied for a whole lifetime! And the more they learn about their host country, the more exciting the pursuit becomes.

Content Coverage

Before the specific subject matter coverage of intercultural training is indicated, it is necessary to discuss a more fundamental issue. Years ago, as the field of intercultural training was developing, the loudest argument to be heard was about whether intercultural training should prepare a person to function in one specific country or whether it could and should prepare someone generically to be able to adapt easily to any country or culture he or she might ever encounter. I am happy to report this argument has long since been settled, through trial and error, and now there is general agreement as to the most effective approach.

Today, every major practitioner begins with generic training, to make the trainees aware of their own ethnocentrism and their enculturation into their own culture, while at the same time, others have been enculturated into their own very different cultures. The starting point for American trainees is usually around the articulation of American values and explicit cultural assumptions. Although it sounds easy enough, and although each of us has been thoroughly drilled in American values, we have never been asked to list them, nor have we even identified them specifically as American values. We thought, instead, we had been taught not the American way, but *the right way, the human way, the way any intelligent, right-thinking person anywhere in the world would do it, given half a chance.*

After this awareness has been achieved, the intercultural training program should move deliberately and systematically into country-specific contrasts and comparisons.

The bulk of the training program, from this point will then concentrate on country-specific training.

The subject matter content for any intercultural training program should include.

1. *Generic indoctrination.*
   - Ethnocentrism (and how to move beyond its confines)
   - The *culture concept* (which will enable us to observe all cultures in a relatively bias-free way)
   - Awareness of our own enculturation
   - What American values and implicit cultural assumptions look like
   - Culture shock (and how to live through it)

2. *Logistical information.* This section is deliberately placed before area studies, because until these questions are answered and these concerns are allayed, trainees find it difficult to concentrate on other matters.
   - What to take with you to the country (and what can be obtained there)
   - Setting up a household in-country
   - Living off the local economy
   - Visa and passport requirements
   - Residence and work documents
   - Legal requirements
   - Housing
   - Utilities/appliances
   - Electric current
   - Weights and measures
   - Mail
   - Telephones, cables, faxes, etc.
   - Transportation
   - Banking
   - Insurance
   - Schools
   - Currency
   - Climate/weather
   - Legal holidays
   - Servants and services
   - Survival needs
   - Support systems
   - Making friends
   - Establishing a daily routine
   - Finding where to buy whatever you need
   - Entertaining
   - Leisure activities

- Mutually supportive family behaviors
- Making new ties for children
- Maintaining old ties

3. *Area studies* (including factual data concerning the host country). Although this section occupies a very small part of this outline, it will consume the largest block of the training program.

    - Demographic data
    - Ethnic composition
    - Historical
    - Geographic
    - Political
    - Economic
    - Education System
    - Religious/philosophical
    - Aesthetic
    - Inventions and scientific achievements
    - Sports and games
    - Places of scenic and historic interest

4. *Language study.* This is generally part of the pre-departure training program only if it is two weeks or more in length; otherwise, language study will begin in-country.

5. *Nonverbal communication* (including the gestures and other paralinguistic considerations that accompany the spoken language).

6. *Family health considerations.*

    - Any health considerations specific to the country (for example, malaria, cholera)
    - Meeting the family's medical needs
    - Where to find a doctor, hospital, and so forth
    - What medications to take along

7. *Social dos and don'ts* (including sensitive topics to be avoided).

8. *Business practices and procedures* (including what motivates host country nationals).

9. *Psycho-cultural differences.*

    - National character traits (for all major ethnic groups within the country)
    - Values
    - Implicit cultural assumptions
    - Thought processes (e.g., inductive or deductive reasoning)

10. *Current problems faced by the people of the country.*

11. *Special problems that most expatriates experience.*

12. *Security and safety issues* (if relevant to the country of assignment).

Instructional strategies and techniques

When intercultural training first began, it took a purely cognitive, intellectual, information-oriented approach. It was *area studies*, following the classical, university-based model, and concentrating, for example, on such information as the *average annual rainfall in Botswana.* In the late 1960s, the more humanistic influences of sensitivity training and the encounter group movement made inroads into intercultural training, and the emphasis shifted to the individual being trained. Trainers then moved to the opposite extreme and often became reluctant to give any specific information about the culture of the country to which the trainee was going. They were interested only in producing people who could *learn how to learn.*

Neither extreme worked very well. Since then, the field has matured a great deal, and as with the generic versus specific argument discussed earlier, it has moved in the direction of incorporating the best features of both approaches as the need for *both* content and process has been realized. The resulting blend has proved much more effective in minimizing culture shock and in maximizing the graduate's productivity in the new cultural setting. In addition to combining the informational and experiential approaches, intercultural trainers are, today, much more conscious of how their training is sequenced and much more responsive to the need to provide a rich variety of training techniques. Another recent development is the purposeful inclusion of stressful situations, which are built into several points of the program, and the attempt to help the trainee learn to live more comfortably with ambiguity. Sometimes the trainer is intentionally confrontational, in order to cause the trainees to question their own assumptions and to inoculate the trainees against failure in the new environment.

For all these reasons, intercultural training uses a variety of approaches, techniques, and methodologies. Standard favorites are case studies, critical incidents, role play, and simulations.

More and more, too, the emphasis has moved from teaching the behaviors observable in the external culture (ending up often with a list of dos and don'ts) to the internal culture, to those things that are not observable on the surface—values, thought patterns, belief systems, and implicit cultural assumptions. These are part of what intercultural specialists are calling deep culture. They are much more difficult to get at, but well worth all the extra trouble it takes to do so.

Several books that include a large variety of training exercises are available.[3]

Evaluation

Since the underlying assumption of this entire chapter is that the user should identify an independent consultant or an institution already prepared to deliver intercultural training, let us discuss evaluation, first of all, in terms of evaluating prospective trainers. This should be done by checking the early-return rate among alumni of the institution delivering the training. In addition, ask for referrals to the directors of international human resources management and development of client companies and place phone calls to discuss their satisfaction or dissatisfaction with the contractor.

Another point of evaluation comes when you have made a tentative selection and have asked that contractor to design a program for you. By looking at the proposal, in

---

[3]See L. Robert Kohls and John M. Knight (1994), *Developing intercultural awareness,* Yarmouth, ME: Intercultural Press; or Sandra M. Fowler and Monica Mumford (1995), *Intercultural sourcebook.* Yarmouth, ME: Intercultural Press.

comparison with the content suggested in this chapter, you can pinpoint omissions in the firm's design.

Finally, ask to sit in on the first workshop being presented for your employees and make your own appraisal of the program. Then discuss your evaluation directly with the contractor.

If you are developing your own in-house intercultural training program, do not be satisfied with the usual end-of-the-course-checklist type of evaluation. In addition to that, follow up with a field evaluation after the alumni have been in the field 1½ years. This timing, although somewhat longer than most follow-up periods, is very important because it is planned so as to fall in a relatively neutral part of the adjustment cycle, thus avoiding periods of unnatural elation or depression.

If your intercultural training is successful, it should greatly reduce the number of early returns and all the related relocation costs. That is the *bottom line,* and it provides a relatively easy way to evaluate the efficacy of your intercultural training program. Effective intercultural training will definitely save your company money.

Summary

Intercultural training is both necessary and readily available for all personnel assigned to serve in foreign countries. It should be required for all overseas transfers and should be given not only to all employees assigned abroad but also to their spouses and all teenage children who will accompany them on the foreign tour. All foreign personnel coming to live and work in the United States also need such preparation, as do all support staff working in the international personnel division of U.S. headquarters office.

Intercultural training is most often provided shortly before the employee's departure (pre-departure training), but several additional options are available as well and ought to be considered. These include an in-country support team to meet the new arrivals and make sure their immediate needs are met and that they get off to a positive start (in-country relocation assistance program) and a training intervention to prepare the employee, psychologically, at the end of the tour, to return to the United States (reentry training).

Four Traditional Approaches to Developing Cross-Cultural Preparedness in Adults:

Education, Training, Orientation, and Briefing

L. Robert Kohls

ABSTRACT: This paper draws a sharp distinction between four contemporary approaches to preparing adults to function in another culture—education, training, orientation, and briefing—and attempts to define each one much more precisely than is usually done, even by specialists. In this way terms that are used very haphazardly in the field are given more clarity, and definitive differences in the four learning modes can be seen as each mode is discovered to have its own distinctive strengths and shortcomings. Each of the four modes is examined in terms of major application, overall purpose, various means of achieving its purpose(s), delivery requirements, and strongest features.

The author argues that once these differences are clearly understood, the designer of the learning experience should then be encouraged to combine the four modes creatively and effectively, rather than being a purist who will use only one mode, thinking it always superior to all the others. He argues that combinations of the various modes are often most effective in real life learning situations. Having made that argument, the author then indicates which aspects of conventional intercultural content seem to fit most naturally within the parameters of each of the four modes under discussion. Finally, a brief description of an existing cross-cultural program presented in each of the four approaches is provided.

Like the proverbial centipede who does not require an advanced degree in engineering to move its hundred legs in perfect synchronization, we do not need to know the technical differences between *training* and *orientation* to help people from one culture adjust to a different culture. On the other hand, it also serves no useful purpose for specialists in the field to use these terms ambiguously or interchangeably. It may, in fact, be an indication of the maturing of the field that we feel a need to define the various approaches to cross-cultural preparation more precisely. In addition to clarifying terminology, we also need to examine the appropriateness of each approach in preparing people to interact with those who are so different from ourselves.

There is a plethora of writing on every aspect of training—approaches, goals, objectives, methodologies—both in and out of the field of intercultural training, and this previous work must be acknowledged. I am not suggesting, with this paper, a new, global, or definitive taxonomy. Rather, I am merely attempting to clarify the definitions of four terms commonly used and misused in the field today, and to suggest that, as defined here, they describe four different current and valid approaches to preparing adults for cross-

Source: (1986). *International Journal of Intercultural Relations,* Vol. 11, Number 1.

cultural assignments.

In discussing education, training, orientation, and briefing, it is apparent that no generic term exists to describe the multiplicity of learning-study approaches we are attempting to categorize. The absence of such a term is probably the reason even specialists in the field use the four terms imprecisely or interchangeably. Therefore I will use the words *learning modes* in this paper to describe these various approaches.

The differences between *education* and *training* have often been contrasted and compared, both in the literature and in the field, over the last two decades. The classical and still most definitive comparison of these two learning modes is presented by Harrison and Hopkins (1967) in their article, *The design of cross-cultural training: An alternative to the university model*. Gudykunst and Hammer (1983) summarize the distinctions between education and training as preparation for their article on the design of intercultural training.

Today, as university professors have become more comfortable with using training techniques such as role plays and case studies in their classrooms, the distinctions between education and training have blurred. Many activities and structured exercises formerly associated with training are now borrowed freely by educators. In this writer's view, the borrowing of such techniques should be further encouraged. And as *educational technology* replaces the *teacher training* approach of the past, we can even hope that the two disciplines of education and training may eventually merge.

Orientation and *briefing* are both terms which have generally been used as alternate words to mean much the same as *training* in the inaccurate yet common parlance of trainers. Orientation and briefing have not previously been compared to either education or training as is done in this paper. The literature on orientation and briefing is practically nonexistent in the way in which these two terms are being used here. The aim of this paper is to use all four terms to have much more precise meanings, each mutually excluding the other three as they are narrowly defined in the context of this paper.

In an attempt to identify and clarify differences among these various terms, we will examine each of the four learning modes—education, training, orientation, and briefing—in terms of (a) major concern or application, (b) overall purpose, (c) various means of achieving its purpose, (d) average time requirements for completion, (e) delivery requirements, and (f) strongest features.

After this analysis of each mode's characteristics has been made, the standard content of cross-cultural preparation is then looked at to determine which pieces seem to fit most naturally in each of the four modes (Section G).

Section H takes all of the previous data (generated in Sections A through G) and combines it in chart form[4] to recapitulate the points already made, and also for greater ease in comparing one specific aspect across all the modes or in looking at any single mode across all its aspects (vertically).

Section I features exemplary cross-cultural programs which fit into each of the four learning modes.

The final section (Section J) identifies important questions to ask in choosing the proper mode to meet a client's particular learning needs.

---

[4]In this book, the chart in Section H has been removed and presented separately on pages 9 to 11.

A. MAJOR CONCERN OR APPLICATION OF EACH MODE

We need to stop thinking how to *prove* that one learning mode is better than another. On the contrary, we should examine each mode for its unique strengths, weaknesses, and applicability to the learning requirements of any given situation. With this positive approach, each mode is of value when the audience and the conditions are appropriate. There is a growing emphasis on using multiple training methodologies and, indeed, it is to our advantage to flexibly shift from mode to mode as the situation dictates. Paige and Martin (1983) suggest moving from the familiar toward the unfamiliar and from the cognitive toward the affective in sequencing this mix of activities.

Education is well suited for relating large bodies of content knowledge and developing in-depth mastery of one or more subjects, whereas *training* usually focuses on *process* and/or on developing competency in performing specific skills or meeting specified objectives in a cost-effective manner (Gudykunst and Hammer, 1983; Harrison and Hopkins, 1967).

Orientation prepares a person to understand and function effectively in a new or radically different environment, and to achieve this shift in the least traumatic manner. *Briefing* provides a broad overview, or it can focus on a particular part of a larger program, in the most time-effective way (since it presents only the most salient features and eliminates all the rest from consideration).

B. OVERALL PURPOSE OF EACH MODE

Education has as its overall purpose the full development of the mind's capabilities, as well as the imparting or acquiring of knowledge—sometimes for no other purpose than for the sheer joy of learning.

On the other hand, the purpose of training is to provide practical, results-oriented learning. This aim has often been applied to a professional, vocational or military context. Generally, a training program is aimed at achieving predetermined and clearly stated objectives which are then measured to determine whether they have been met.

Orientation's purpose is to *orient* a person to a place or position, especially to new situations, environments, ideas, values, or operating principles. Orientation helps a person understand how to operate comfortably in an unfamiliar setting, such as how to hail a taxi or summon a waiter, or to know what are acceptable topics for *small talk* conversation with someone to whom you have just been introduced.

Briefing's purpose is to provide the background of an organization, topic, place or situation in a concise and focused format, giving the most essential information in a very limited time span and emphasizing or highlighting certain points or features.

C. MEANS OF ACHIEVING THAT PURPOSE

Any of the learning modes can use an unlimited number of methodologies to achieve their ends; at the same time, their *carriers* (i.e., the people delivering them) can even invent new ones if they are particularly creative and experienced. Consequently, no learning modes can be restricted to a specific set of activities. The following, however are drawn from those activities traditionally associated with each mode.

Education achieves its purpose through the teacher, often serving as a role model, who passes on knowledge (or a particular specialization or approach) to the student. In addition to lecture-presentations, the teacher often uses question-and-answer sessions, reading assignments, written assignments and periodic examinations.

Training uses *experiential* and participant-centered exercises, emphasizing *hands on* experience, practice, and drills to achieve its purpose. Training has access to an extensive repertoire of highly developed methodologies to accomplish a variety of clearly designated ends (see Batchelder and Warner, 1977; Casse, 1979; Casse, 1982; Hoopes and Ventura, 1979; Kohls, 1979; Kohls, 1981; Landis and Brislin, 1983; Paige and Martin, 1983; Pusch, 1979; Wight and Hammons, 1970; Weeks, Pedersen, and Brislin, 1977).

Orientation programs meet their goals by helping participants shift from their old orientation to a new one by starting *where they are* at the point of entry and introducing them to approaches which are more appropriate in the new environment. Orientation draws on methodologies borrowed from training and education.

Briefing achieves its purpose by systematically presenting cogent, highly organized, simplified and sequenced information, often in chart form, and usually followed by a question-and-answer session to clear up any ambiguous or misunderstood points.

D. AVERAGE AMOUNT OF TIME REQUIRED TO COMPLETE EACH MODE

Throughout, this paper lists the four learning modes from the longest-to-shortest time required to achieve the mode's purpose.

Education is the longest-term of the four modes. It is now popular to consider it a life-long activity. *Formal education*, however, is more often defined as completed upon receipt of an undergraduate university or college degree. Education is frequently divided into segments such as courses, class periods, semesters, grade levels or years.

Training programs vary greatly in duration. Most commonly, they last one day to one or two weeks, but a sequenced training schedule with a number of separate courses can last from three to six months.

Orientation programs are usually from one-half day to one week in length.

Briefings can be as short as 10 to 15 minutes or can last an hour or an hour and a half.

E. WHO DELIVERS EACH MODE?

Descriptive titles have commonly been used to indicate who delivers learning modes, but delivery is by no means restricted to these people.

Education, for example, is taught by educators, teachers, professors of various ranks, or teaching fellows (graduate students).

Training is done by trainers or facilitators. In a successful training session, learning points are also made by the trainees themselves, who learn from their peers or fellow participants. Also, the training mode tends to use subject-experts in the development of the training program, but not in its presentation or delivery.

Orientation has not developed specific names to describe the people who deliver the programs. *Orientators* sounds artificial and is seldom used in practice. Instead, a functional title, such as *program coordinator*, is most often used, depending on the program or orientation. *Session leader* is also a commonly used term.

Briefings are delivered by an expert (or by cadre in a military situation) on any particular topic. These experts are usually incumbents in in-house positions whose job descriptions indicate one of their duties to be to give briefings on their area(s) of expertise on a periodic, *as needed*, or emergency basis.

F. STRONGEST FEATURES OF EACH MODE

At the beginning of this paper I made the argument that no single learning mode is superior to another in an absolute sense. However, each mode is uniquely suited or unsuited, given an audience of a particular profile and a particular set of conditions; as a result, one mode can be said to be superior to another for a particular situation. Therefore, it is useful to examine each mode individually for its strengths and unique features.

Education can be most thorough in its coverage, since time is not a major factor when considering education as a *lifetime activity* or formal education as routinely lasting four or twelve years. The educational approach is generally used in delivering large bodies of content information. Another strength of education is its effectiveness in the theoretical realm and in focusing, in depth, on a specialized subfield. Education is, however, the most passive of the four modes and may sometimes be the most boring, in that there is little active participation by the learner.

Training is the most active and *involving* of all the modes. It is also the most cost-effective since it often has designed into it an evaluation component to determine whether the learning objectives were met. Trainees (*participants*) contribute to their own learning, thus gaining content information, skill in applying the information or skills learned, and self-confidence at the same time. Training is perhaps the most effective of the modes in the development of predetermined performance skills.

Orientation is the most supportive of the modes, for it does not remove the participant's original orientation framework until the new one is firmly established. It transforms while minimizing the shock of the foreign environment.

Briefings are the most time-effective mode. They achieve the maximum amount of information transfer in the shortest possible time. Also, they spotlight the most relevant and essential information so the recipient is not required to sort out the essential from the nonessential.

G. EXAMPLES OF APPROPRIATE INTERCULTURAL CONTENT FITTING INTO EACH MODE

Up to this point, all information provided on the four modes is equally applicable to all fields of content knowledge. To show the relevance of each mode to the discipline of intercultural communication, this section looks—mode by mode—at those aspects of the field which fit most naturally into each. Since it is assumed that the reader is already familiar with intercultural terms and concepts, detailed definitions are not provided.

The most obvious example of a topic from our field which is usually presented in the *education* mode is area studies (with its division into historic, political, economic, social, and aesthetic subcategories). Language acquisition, often an inseparable companion to area studies, also is taught most often in the educational mode.

A generic concept often presented in a *training* mode is cultural awareness. So, too, are specific skills (e.g., *The participants will interpret a short videotaped scenario from dual perspectives: (a) that of a typical middle-class American, as compared with (b) a traditional person from country X*).

Several types of information fit most comfortably into the orientation mode:

1. Practical information concerning specific survival skills (e.g., using the bus or subway by yourself, finding and arranging to rent an apartment, shopping for groceries, enrolling your children in school, surviving an American winter—if you are from a tropical country).

2. Customs (with emphasis on differences).

3. Institutions—both the *large* ones (e.g., the political system or the educational system) and the *small* ones (e.g., the family, marriage and divorce, the women's movement, male-female relationships).

Other concepts that lend themselves well to being presented in an orientation mode are the subjects of values and comparative values.

The briefing mode works well in providing a broad overview of the field, relevant background information that should be taken into account, or descriptions of current situations.

These specific examples, all of which might logically be part of any one program, substantiate the desirability of shifting from mode to mode, rather than maintaining strict adherence to any single mode.

H. COMPARISON OF THE FOUR MODES, ASPECT FOR ASPECT

In order to review the various points we have made thus far and to make it easier to compare all of the characteristics within any single mode, as well as to compare one particular aspect across modes, the salient points made in defining each learning mode have been displayed in chart form. [See pages 9 to 11 of this book.]

I. OUTSTANDING EXAMPLE OF A PROGRAM IN EACH LEARNING MODE

By briefly describing an outstanding example of a recognized program in each of the learning modes, various points made in this paper may be clarified and reinforced. Specific examples will show practical applications of the theoretical matters heretofore discussed.

Education Example

Country-specific programs designed to prepare American business people for overseas assignments are presented by the Business Council for International Understanding (BCIU), associated with American University, in Washington, D.C. BCIU, now more than 25 years old, is headquartered in New York City, and has its training office in Washington, D.C., where most but not all of the training takes place. BCIU, will, on request, carry training to any site.

Mid- and upper-level executives from America's Fortune 500 corporations are enrolled in BCIU programs tailored to their time requirement and operational needs. For the most part, corporate personnel who participate in these programs have just received their first overseas assignment.

A typical program lasts one week, and BCIU contracts as many as 15 country experts to make presentations. Content sessions are sometimes also held during meal and evening hours. Although programs can be developed for any size group, most are presented to a single executive and spouse because most overseas placements are assigned one at a time. (Individual programs make the BCIU program relatively expensive, yet infinitely less costly than bringing an executive and family home early because they could not adjust.) Most sessions are presented in the lecture format. After the specialist summarizes the subject, participants are given a chance to ask questions about anything left unanswered or unclear.

All BCIU courses include one session which is in a training rather than an educational mode—an open-ended role play with a foreigner whose value system is diametrically opposed to mainstream American values. The corporate executives who go through BCIU's programs will live a rather luxurious lifestyle in their country of assignment, with servants, country club memberships, and many other perquisites.

Training Example

The U.S. Peace Corps has prepared its volunteers by using the training approach since 1965, when the Westinghouse Learning Corporation won its first Peace Corps training contract. Prior to 1965 the Peace Corps used an area studies (or educational) approach. Today, most training is done in-country. The Peace Corps provided the funds and the testing grounds for the first large-scale experiential cross-cultural training in this country. Many of the leading cross-cultural trainers active today learned their own skills on Peace Corps training staff assignments.

Peace Corps volunteers are of all ages and professional levels, but the majority of them are young men and women, often recently graduated from college and idealistic yet practical in their orientation. In the early years of the Corps most were B. A. generalists; now most come with vocational skills. The typical volunteer has little or no work experience, is open minded, flexible, and willing to live at a minimal standard of living for a two year assignment. All are sent to Third World, *developing* nations with low GNPs.

Orientation Example

The Washington International Center (WIC) in Washington, D.C., has used the orientation mode since its inception 35 years ago. The U.S. State Department, unable to find a ready-made program to prepare official foreign visitors invited to visit the United States, asked the American Council on Education to create a private institution to design such a program. As a result, the world's oldest institution designed to facilitate cross-cultural understanding was established.

In its early years, WIC's visitors were all from the former enemy nations of Germany and Japan; the program was soon broadened to accommodate participants coming through the Marshall Plan. Today, the Agency for International Development (AID), the successor to the Marshall Plan, is WIC's major sponsor. AID invites mainly mid-level bureaucrats from Third World countries to receive advanced education or training in the United States. Most visitors are male; about 15% are female. Nearly 150,000 people from more than 150 different countries are alumni of the program.

For most participants, WIC is the first stop on their first trip to the United States. Typical participants expect to receive a certain respectful acknowledgment of their rank—because they are used to receiving it at home and because they are the official, invited guests of the United States Government. However, they need to be prepared to associate with American citizens who will not give them any more respect than they give anyone else. Although all are mature adults, this is likely to be the first time many of them have been *on their own* in a foreign country. Their traditional values are probably exactly opposite to the basic American values. They need considerable support while being prepared to function in a culture which is close to 180 degrees from their own. WIC's orientation program is available every week of the year.

Briefing Example

The Overseas Briefing Center at the Foreign Service Institute of the U.S Department of State is perhaps the best example of a cross-cultural briefing program. Foreign Service officers and their spouses, preparing to be posted at U.S. Embassies around the world, are the principal users of this service. Many already have several years of overseas experience; now they need current resources for country-specific information to prepare, in the shortest time possible, for their next postings.

Individuals need to have access to the data bank in their own time frames, to accommodate their hectic schedules as they prepare to leave for their country of assignment. The Briefing Center maintains active and accurate information on 250 posts around the world in a variety of media, (including print media, slide shows, and videotapes). In addition, the Center keeps a file on recent returnees from each post who are willing to be *on call* as human information resources. Although developed for the use of U.S. diplomats, the services are also available for *walk in* use by any citizen.

J. IMPORTANT QUESTIONS TO ASK IN CHOOSING THE PROPER LEARNING MODES

This section covers questions to ask when determining the best-suited learning mode (or combination of modes) for any specific situation. The questions that follow form the basis of a Needs Assessment; they are meant to serve as examples rather than being considered exhaustive:

1. What is the composite profile of the participants? (age, sex, rank, social status, educational level, customary learning mode in their country, etc.)
2. What are the objectives of the learning; what are its final goals and uses?
3. How closely can the participants be expected to be associated with the foreign culture after the learning is completed?
4. What is the maximum amount of pre-departure time available to prepare participants for the cross-cultural experience?
5. Which parts of the preparation are to be completed prior to departure?
6. Which learning activities can be continued after participants arrive in-country?
7. How similar is the cultural pattern of the participant's native country to the target country?
8. Where will the learning take place? (physical setting)
9. How flexible, experimental and open to change is the learning population judged to be?
10. What are the budgetary restrictions/limitations?
11. What are the staff resources; how adaptable is the staff?
12. What are the expectations/requirements/restrictions of the sponsoring agency?

There are, of course, no magic questions to ask and no hard-and-fast rules which can be applied universally to lead one to always choose one training mode over all others in any given set of circumstances. At best such decisions may seem to the impartial observer to be made on the basis of intuition rather than on solid empirical evidence. Yet there are guidelines and generalizations which can be stated in relation to the above questions and the decisions which they are designed to elicit.

For example, younger participants and those with higher intellects and more previous formal education tend to respond more favorably to the inductive and experiential activities of training methodologies. But when time is a major consideration, it must be conceded that it takes approximately twice as long to present the same amount of content experientially as it does didactically. (How much is actually retained is another matter.)

Since the amount of content delivered is extremely limited in the briefing mode and its overall process is a deductive one, this mode will likely be appropriate where time restrictions are greatest.

Another factor to consider is that most older participants, as well as those from Third World countries whose previous educational experience has been entirely through rote memorization, have more faith in the processes of education than they do in those of training. Consequently, all else being equal, the education mode may be chosen for them. It may still be decided to use the training mode, however if such participants are being prepared, later, to enter American training sessions in their specialization. To make the transition from their original expectations to their future needs will require a carefully sequenced introduction of gradually more and more *threatening* exercises and a proportionally greater amount of time.

To the extent that behavioral goals have been set, and to the extent that they have been well conceptualized, training, or some combination in which the training approach is dominant, is probably indicated, since training generally does a better job of fulfilling clearly delineated goals. The obvious exception to this would be where the ultimate objective is for the participant to pass an examination proving that a sizable body of knowledge has been mastered. In that case, the education mode would probably be most effective.

Staffs, if they are pre-existent rather than selected to fill a particular need, and client organizations, if they attempt to wield more power than their experience merits, may also be the determining factors in selecting one particular mode over another.

Compromise may even enter the equation. Where a training approach is preferred by those who are delivering the learning-experience and where an education approach is demanded by those who are buying the services, the orientation approach may end up providing the most acceptable solution.

These are only the barest indications of how one would use these and other questions to determine which combination of learning modes to use in any particular situation, but it is hoped these few guidelines may be sufficient to lead the reader into making his or her own decisions, based on something more than intuition alone.

To further illustrate why the above questions should be asked in determining the unique needs of any learning group, three case studies are included for the reader's analysis.

CASE STUDY I

You have been appointed the Facilitator for a mixed group of Japanese and American educators who are meeting on the west coast for an intensive one week program to discuss and define the essential similarities and differences between the two cultures.

The Japanese in the group seem very satisfied to listen to lectures which attempt to catalog the similarities and differences. They appear to be the only ones who are madly taking notes during such lectures. The more specific the lists they are able to produce, the happier they are with the session.

The Americans have become restive from what they think have been too many sessions of listening to long-winded experts. They are pressing for more open discussions and are suggesting ideas for experiential activities they want you to include in the schedule.

Whenever you've tried open discussions, only the Americans hold forth with their opinions and argue with each other, trying to persuade the group of the validity of their proposed theories. The Japanese sit quietly through such sessions as if they should wait to be called upon before participating. But no one calls upon them. The Americans are so interested in arguing their points of view that they seem not to have noticed the one-sidedness of the participation.

You're well aware of the two very different modes of operating, and you'd like to find some way to facilitate real communication between the two groups, but you don't know what to suggest.

You've called together a special planning session composed of three of the more articulate Japanese and three of the more sensitive Americans to discuss the problem and to brainstorm solutions.

CASE STUDY II

You are in charge of a one week *Orientation to America* program for 25 foreign graduate students newly arrived from 20 different countries in Europe, Latin America, Asia, and Africa. You and your assistant have planned what you consider to be an exciting, involving program. Its heavy emphasis on experiential learning techniques has been designed to get the trainees out into the community so they can learn from their actual experiences.

The program has just begun and you are somewhat troubled. In your estimation, your first meeting, which you had planned as a group discussion (in which you had hoped to gain the commitment of all the trainees), fell flat. Only the students from Western Europe and India became involved to the degree you had wanted. The East Asian and Southeast Asian students were particularly quiet. The African students looked as though they didn't know what was going on.

You are trying to figure out what you can do to activate those who are the most shy and to get the group to function as a unit. What will you try?

CASE STUDY III

You are an experienced American teacher-trainer who became very excited when you learned you would become involved in your first overseas training adventure—training a rather large group of 30 to 40 year old male Egyptian middle school teachers in Cairo.

Now that you are two and one half weeks into the six week training program, you're not so happy you came. Things are not going at all well. You've tried everything you can think of—role-play (your specialty), case studies (you even tried to get them to write up their own problem experiences as case studies so they would be realistic enough), and several different group exercises which have always worked so well with your American student teachers.

The group seems particularly uncooperative and surly. Even when you publicly and persistently urge one of them to respond, he reluctantly and half-heartedly gives only a minimal grunt or nod of his head, and the whole group then exchanges nasty, knowing glances at each other.

Privately, several of the members have come to ask you when the teaching is going to begin. When you replied, *It's already begun; this is a new approach, I'm not going to be lecturing to you,* they seemed confused. Some or them even became openly critical. Now the open hostility within the group frightens you.

You are convinced there is more than ample experience within the group which all would benefit from if you could only find some way to get them to loosen up and share their knowledge and experience.

You've tried everything you can think of, and you're exhausted. One more request for a lecture, and you're likely to explode!

What will you try next?

In analyzing these three cases, the reader may find it helpful, after reading all three carefully, to ask (in addition to the initial list of questions in Section J) these specific questions:

- What are the similarities in the three cases?
- What are the differences?
- How can the *problem* in each case be stated in a simple sentence?
- What is the composition of each group?
- Where will the participants work after the initial program is finished?
- What is the group's expectation of the program?
- How does the group expect the leader to act?
- In each situation, who are the foreigners?
- What would you suggest as *solutions* in each of the cases?
- Case by case, will you likely suggest an education, training, orientation, or briefing approach?
- For which one of the three situations does a highly experiential approach seem justified, and why?

SUMMARY

All of the learning modes—education, training, orientation, and briefing—have their strengths and limitations. The characteristics of the learning group and the sponsoring agency's requirements should determine the most effective modes in any particular case. A carefully selected mixture of modes, flexibly determined by the staff who facilitate the learning, can provide a more effective learning experience.

REFERENCES

Batchelder, D., and Warner, E. 1977. *Beyond experience: The experiential approach to cross-cultural education*. Brattleboro, VT: The Experiment Press.

Casse, Pierre. 1979. *Training for the cross-cultural mind*. Washington, DC: SIETAR.

———. 1982. *Training for the multicultural manager*. Washington, DC: SIETAR.

Gudykunst, W., and Hammer, M. 1983. "Basic training design: Approaches to intercultural training." In Donald Landis and Richard Brislin (Eds.), *Handbook of Intercultural Training* (Vol. I, pp. 118-154). New York, NY: Pergamon Press.

Harrison, Roger, and Hopkins, Richard L. 1967. "The design of cross-cultural training: An alternative to the university model." *Journal of Applied Behavioral Sciences* III (4), 431-461.

Hoopes. David, and Ventura, Paul (Eds.). 1979. *Intercultural sourcebook: cross-cultural training methodologies*. Washington, DC: SIETAR.

Kohls, L. Robert. 1979. *Methodologies for trainers: a compendium of learning strategies*. Washington, DC: Future Life Press.

————. 1981. *Developing intercultural awareness*. Washington, DC: SIETAR.

Landis, Donald, and Brislin, Richard. (Eds.) 1983. *Handbook of Intercultural Training* (Vol. 1, II, and III). New York, NY: Pergamon Press.

Paige, R. Michael, and Martin, J. 1983. "Ethical issues and ethics in cross-cultural training." In Donald Landis and Richard Brislin (Eds.), *Handbook of intercultural training* (Vol. 1. pp. 36-60). New York, NY: Pergamon Press.

Pusch, Margaret. 1979. *Multicultural Education: A cross-cultural approach*. Yarmouth, ME: Intercultural Press.

Weeks, William, Pedersen, Paul, and Brislin, Richard. (Eds.). 1977. *A manual of structured experiences for cross-cultural learning*. Washington, DC: SIETAR.

Wight, Albert P., and Hammons, M. 1970. *Guidelines for Peace Corps cross-cultural training*. (4 vols.) Estes Park, CO: Center for Research and Education (Out of print, but available through ERIC).

KINDS OF CROSS-CULTURAL TRAINING AVAILABLE

L. Robert Kohls

Relocation training

Initial on-site support

Re-entry training and repatriation counseling

Managing diversity in the work force

Supervisory skills for diverse employees

Multinational team-building

Intercultural awareness training

Intercultural communication skills for managers

Management training in international organizations

Joint-venture preparation

International human resources management

Americanization training for foreign nationals

International negotiation facilitation

Protocol to receive international representatives

Please see "Intercultural Training for Overseas Posting," pages 15-30 of this book, for full descriptions.

WHAT INTERCULTURAL TRAINING WILL DO

L. Robert Kohls

The cross-cultural training program will equip the employee to do several things to insure the expatriate's overseas survival:

1. Prepare for the physical move overseas.

2. Master the logistical skills of surviving in the foreign country (e.g., marketing, housing, transportation, schooling).

3. Communicate, verbally and non verbally, with nationals of the country.

4. Make a minimum number of social blunders in the new environment.

5. Make sense of a totally different set of operative values, implicit assumptions, and an unfamiliar reasoning process and system of logic.

6. Apply the indigenous values, implicit assumptions, reasoning process and logic system (rather than one's own) to interpret all that is seen and heard in the new culture.

7. Successfully weather the trauma of culture shock (which, while we haven't spoken of it yet in this booklet, is very real and very debilitating, and must be dealt with).

8. Facilitate a rapid and successful adjustment for each family member to the host culture, and enable all of them to have a positive, productive overseas experience.

9. Move toward becoming bicultural, and, eventually, if the newcomer lives in the foreign country long enough, to become fully bicultural (i.e., able to function comfortably in more than one cultural mode of operation).

10. And, as a side benefit, help the employee to better understand his/her own culture—and him/herself.

Source: L. Robert Kohls. (1974). *Intercultural training: don't leave home without it.* Washington, DC: SIETAR.

CONTENT AND SEQUENCING OF CROSS-CULTURAL TRAINING

© 1985 L. Robert Kohls

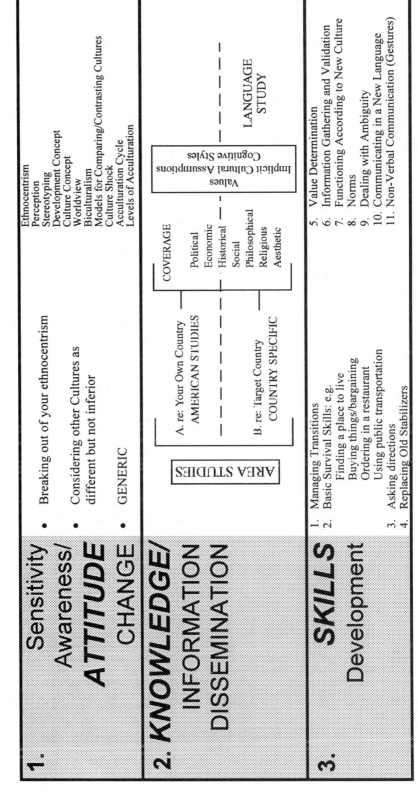

SEVEN ISSUES IN CROSS-CULTURAL TRAINING

L. Robert Kohls

This paper presents seven issues which I consider to be the most important ones in the cross-cultural training field today. Some of these issues derive from ethical concerns; others relate to professional standards. The issues are:

1. **Different approaches are appropriate for different cultures.** Stated another way, the current American approach to training is radical and absolutely inappropriate for seven-eighths of the world.

Let me illustrate the point by comparing the current American approach with the reactions and expectations of a more Traditional society:[1]

The Current American Approach Holds that:	A More *Traditional* Society Would Likely Expect:
1. The trainees are responsible for their own learning. They should determine what they need to learn.	The trainer should be the expert, and he/she should act the part. He/she should tell the trainees what they need to know. The trainees couldn't assess their own needs even if they wanted to. How could they *know what they don't know?* To admit they didn't already know anything would be to admit they had shortcomings and would cause a loss of *face*.
2. Training objectives are absolutely crucial in planning and organizing the learning process. Behavioral change can best be accomplished through carefully constructed, behaviorally stated, performance-based objectives.	Establishing training objectives is perceived as a threat by the trainee—for if they were not able to reach those objectives, they would have failed. Besides, clear-cut, written objectives prevent flexibility in the learning process. The only meaningful evaluation is that of the trainer's performance.
3. *Learning by doing* is the most effective technique. Learning through experimentation is strongly encouraged.	Trainees learn by observing the trainer and modeling their behavior on his/hers. *Learning by doing* is too risky and too inefficient. Exercises and simulations make us expose ourselves and make us look foolish. The trainer should tell us (out of his/her experience) the right way to do the things we need to know how to do.

In short, the American approach (reflected in the experiential direction so favored in training) works only for Westerners. Unfortunately, many American trainers do not realize this.

If more than one culture is involved in a training program, these differences must be taken into account.

---

[1] I am indebted to Pierre Casse of the World Bank for these examples.

2. We need to be aware of the hidden but very obtrusive cultural assumptions that underlie all our statements and all our actions.

I will mention only three as examples, but be warned that the cross-cultural training world is riddled with them. HumRRO[2], in developing its *contrast American* approach, identified over 60 such significant differences.

(1) The Concept of Fate

Americans find it difficult even to imagine how seriously most of the world considers the role *Fate* plays in their lives. To us it seems like superstition, to be avoided at all cost. Americans find it both difficult and repugnant to accept the fact that there are some things (actually many things) which lie beyond the power of man to achieve.

Seven-eighths of the world believes religiously in the concept of *Fate*. This all-pervasive concept literally rules their lives. *Fate* controls who you are and what you will become. You can't move out of the social level into which you were born.

Americans on the other hand, don't know this is the case, so they proceed as if *Fate* didn't exist—as if there were no limitations—and move from one level of society to the next higher level, and to the next, and the next.

For many Americans, there is nothing beyond the power of *Man*. We have brought nature into control. Our homes, for example can, through the marvels of air conditioning and central heating, be maintained at the same constant temperature year round, regardless of outside climate. We have literally gone to the moon, because we couldn't accept the limitations that we couldn't. We seem to be challenged to do, by one means or another (and often at great cost), what seven-eighths of the world knows can't be done.

(2) The Concept of Change

We think *Change* is automatically a good thing. *Change*, to us is synonymous with growth, evolution, improvement, development, and progress. Not so with seven-eighths of the world. For seven-eighths of the world, *Change* is not a positive force, not something considered desirable, but a destructive force, and one which should be avoided.

The positive alternatives to *Change* are difficult for most Americans even to imagine, but they are such qualities as stability, continuity, tradition, and a rich and ancient heritage—none of which, incidentally, Americans consider important.

(3) The Concept of Equality

Equality is, for us, one of our most cherished institutions. This concept is so important to Americans that we have even given it a religious basis. To us, all people are equal. It would be difficult, indeed, to prove this purely from the physical evidence. We look around us and see people born with handicaps of all sorts, or we see people with less than half the intelligence we possess, or we see people in every conceivable condition of wretchedness, yet we believe religiously *that all people are equal*.

This concept certainly makes Americans unique.

Seven-eighths of the world feels quite differently. To them, rank and status and authority are much more desirable conditions—even if they happen to find themselves near the bottom of the social heap. It gives people in those societies a sense of security and certainty we are likely never to know. There is something reassuring in knowing,

---

[2]Human Resource Research Organization, Alexandria, Virginia.

from birth, who you are and where you fit into the complex system we call *society*. There is something rewarding, too, in realizing that the services you render are indispensable to that very society.

Seven-eighths of the world's people don't seem to mind showing deference and respect to someone of a higher position the way Americans do.

I have not dealt here with concepts as alien to Americans as Karma or reincarnation, but you can imagine the far-reaching implications of such beliefs.

3. **The Generic vs. Specific Argument.** Of the seven issues mentioned in this paper, this is the one which has stirred the inner circles of cross-cultural trainers for a longer time than any of the others. I am happy to report that there is very little discussion of this once-important issue today. There is now general agreement that both are necessary, and even fairly general agreement as to the best order in which to present these two essential components of cross-cultural training.

The wisdom of this more generous view can easily be seen if one thinks of the generic training as *cross-cultural awareness training* and of the specific training as *country-specific orientation* (or as *area studies* at its best). Then it seems obvious that both are essential.

It is now generally accepted that we should begin with the generic component, to lay the basic foundation. Many trainers even prefer to begin by creating an awareness of what American culture is and how we have all been enculturated as Americans (while others were being enculturated as Greeks or Turks or Japanese).

After this foundation has been laid, other cultures might be contrasted with the American, in a general way, and finally the training program would focus, in ever-increasing detail, on the target country and its indigenous culture.

One further observation is in order before we proceed to the next issue. It is possible, probably even desirable, to provide the generic training here in the U.S. before departing for the foreign country, but it is difficult, if not impossible, to give the specific training before arrival in the host country. Trainees seem incapable of imagining the differences before they actually encounter them.

4. **The Content vs. Process Argument.** This argument is an issue only in that too many cross-cultural trainers feel that process is so all-important that they ignore content altogether. On the other hand, many educators act as though content should be the only concern and the way in which that content is delivered is of little importance. This is the area in which both training and education could learn from the other discipline.

Trainers make the point that content is the easiest part to develop and that many people are able to provide that content. Also, the content, no matter how well developed, will never be gotten across to the trainees if no attention is paid to the process. Hence, process has assumed considerable emphasis in the training field. As important as process is, however, it cannot survive without the content; this is a point too many trainers fail to realize.

What we are calling *process* here has been derived from advances, over the last couple of decades, in group process and human relations work. Without them, there would be no *training* as we know it today.

The trainer functions as a facilitator, coach or guide. It is absolutely essential that every experiential exercise be *processed*. This is best done in the small group context.

5. **The Debate as to *Whether Behavioral Objectives Can or Should Be Imposed onto Cross-Cultural Training.*** To this question the Peace Corps replies with a resounding *Yes*, and has been doing so with some success since 1972.

But many, perhaps most, individual trainers have grave doubts.

I, personally, think the process one goes through in developing training around behavioral or performance-based objectives is so worthwhile that it should be attempted whether the answer to the question is *yes* or *no*.

I also believe it is possible, even if it is very difficult.

The *Cross-Cultural Preparedness Rating Sheet*, which I developed in 1969, presents 42 sets of polar opposites (for a total of 84 points), all stated in performance terms. These are all items which can be observed during the course of the training.[3]

6. **Disincentives to Cross-Cultural Learning.** Only two disincentives will be discussed in this paper.

   (1) The trainees' demand for a list of *Dos and Don'ts* and their all-consuming need to have logistical questions answered *ad infinitum*. This is certain to create a problem when it is coupled with the fact that many trainers are absolutely adamant about not providing such information—because this seems like such a *shallow* approach when they want to help the trainees *learn how to learn*.

   After trying it both ways many times, I am convinced it is best to give such information, to give it early on, and to get it out of the way so you can get on with the real learning—even if it takes two full days. These needs, on the part of the trainees, are real, and they will not go away until they are satisfied. Unmet, they will simply impede the training process.

   (2) The *all people are basically alike* cop-out. This Mr. Magoo attitude is very common and very destructive to cross-cultural understanding (Mr. Magoo could travel to Finland, Albania, Morocco, or Afghanistan and never notice that he was out of the United States.)

   Americans are threatened by differences. (Not all people are.) So we want to see similarities and to see all people as basically alike at the core. The human perceptual processes allow us to see whatever we want to see, so it is a *provable* precept to assume that all people are basically alike and then to begin seeing evidence to support our claim. The problem with such an assumption is that it makes cross-cultural learning most difficult, probably even impossible.

   The only way I have found to combat this very common attitude in American trainees is to force them into and through a kind of culture shock in relation to their own American culture. This process takes some time, and it requires a carefully structured strategy which forces them to realize that one of the things which Americans hold nearest and dearest—our belief in the sanctity of the individual—is, in absolute terms, a hoax. (In *relative* terms, it is, of course, quite significant.) The trainees must be led to *realize* that we, who make so much of our individual differences and individual rights, have been as much shaped by our culture as everyone else in the world; and that each culture's enculturation

---

[3]The process with which it is intended to be used is also very important. It is to be completed first by the trainee and then by the trainer, who fills one out for each trainee. Then the differences in perception become the basis for a private counseling session between the trainer and trainee.

process shapes everybody differently; and that those differences are, indeed, very different—especially if you find yourself in the middle of culture shock in an alien land.

7. The Need for Materials Development. The need for materials for trainers to use is both urgent and massive. It is nothing short of miraculous that trainers have been able to accomplish so much with so few resources. There are needs for training exercises and for materials for both generic and specific training (although most materials which have already been developed have been for generic training).

Two recent attempts have been made to:

(1) Create an overall structure to present the scope of our developmental needs, and

(2) To publicize these needs to the researchers and materials developers, in the hope that they will produce the materials we need so desperately.

The first was a paper that I developed for the Action Caucus at the December 1977 Convention of the Speech Communication Association.[4] The second was a brainstorming session of fifteen cross-cultural trainers at the February 1978 Conference of SIETAR.

The overall impression this paper should convey is that there is hardly a single, homogeneous direction to cross-cultural training as the field celebrates its fifteenth birthday.[5] What has not been conveyed, and should be, is the fervor with which individual trainers argue their convictions and the dedication they evidence in applying themselves so completely to the long hours required by a training program. There is a lot of spirit in the field, even something akin to missionary zeal. It is, without question, one of the most exciting arenas in intercultural communication today.

---

[4] "A Practitioner's View of Research and Materials Development Needs for Training in Intercultural Relations."

[5] This paper was written in 1980. The field of training had its beginning in the mid 1960s. Interestingly enough, training has been associated with intercultural communication and helping people adjust to foreign cultures from its inception.

CARRYING AMERICAN-DESIGNED TRAINING OVERSEAS[6]

L. Robert Kohls

Inductive Training for Deductive Minds:

Round Pegs into Square Holes

> What is this intercultural communications stuff anyway? I've always found that if you dig down deep enough, people are all just people—wherever they come from. You cut 'em and they bleed, whether they come from Germany or Japan or the good ole U.S.A.!
>
> If a person knows his profession, that's all he needs to know to do his job, here or anywhere else in the world.
>
> Don't tell me I have to treat people from other countries like they're something special. Human beings are human beings, and I treat' 'em all alike!

The above quotation is a composite drawn from an attitude which I have heard expressed by American trainers more times than I could count. To me the opinion reveals two characteristics: ignorance and arrogance. Ignorance—because it seems to indicate total unawareness of the radically different learning expectations of most of the world's people. Arrogance—because it only slightly conceals the belief that all things American (and the current *training* approach is very American) are naturally superior.

As the Venezuelan educator Luis Machado has said, *Stupidity is a curable disease*; therefore it will be my task to try to cure that stupidity in this paper. Arrogance is more difficult to handle, and I will leave that for others to accomplish.

Quite obviously, some American trainers (with attitudes not too dissimilar to those expressed in the above quotation) **are** carrying their American-designed training overseas to present it to foreign audiences. And many of them have not noticed that the round pegs are not fitting very well into the square holes. Some, on the other hand, have noticed that the fit hasn't been any too good. Trainer Reginald Smart, Australian by birth and Californian by choice, writes of his attempt a few years ago to carry his Western-developed training to Singapore:

> The expansion of management education to the Third World is happening apace. Enterprising Western trainers who see this as a new market and offer short courses for established managers are received enthusiastically by native company officials who want the competitive advantage of knowing the latest. The indigenous managers who enroll seem so like any other group of managers that intercultural problems are easily overlooked, to the trainer's regret! It seems easy to justify the assumption that what works well in a Western setting will prove to be an effective learning model in an Asian, Arab, African or Latin setting. And when trainees amicably go along with our methods and materials, we tend to accept their conformity with relief. After all, there's enough to do without looking for problems. (But) the use of Western learning models (is far) less effective in the non-

---

[6]Opening Plenary Session at the International Roundtable, The World Bank, Washington, DC, February 7, 1986. Jointly Sponsored by The American Society for Training and Development and The World Bank.

Western world than the politeness and ambition of trainees in non-Western countries would sometimes lead us to believe.[7]

Deductive or Inductive?

At the root of the problem is a fundamental difference in learning expectations. To state it another way, it is a question of whether there is a preference for the inductive or the deductive approach. Just to make sure we have not mixed up these two (as I have so often done) I will redefine them briefly.

Deductive is, for example, when the *professor*, who has all the knowledge of a particular field, comes into the classroom, greets the students, and announces the topic of today's lecture. Then he lists the six principles that provide the basis for all his assumptions, explains them, and finally, he offers several specific examples to illustrate each principle. Meanwhile, the students, who would consider it rude to interrupt the professor with questions, are busy writing down all the golden words which fall from the expert's mouth, so they will be able to regurgitate them on the test later.

Inductive is when the *facilitator* takes the day's topic and turns it into key questions, experiential exercises, group activities and pre-developed handouts, all designed to draw out the group's collective knowledge of the subject, which the facilitator writes on the ever-present flip chart. From this collection of data, the underlying principles of the subject are discovered, under the skillful guidance of the facilitator, so that the trainees feel they have participated in their own learning. The facilitator pulls the whole experience together by *processing* all that has transpired.

Deductive moves from the general to the specific, and inductive moves from the specific to the general. We can also refer to the contrasting deductive and inductive approaches as *didactic* and *experiential*, respectively.

Inductive is, of course, the approach utilized by the American trainer, and we American trainers are so *sold* on the efficacy of the experiential approach that many of us are convinced it is the *best thing since sliced bread*. Why wouldn't we want to take it with us when we go to train the Japanese or the Saudis?

Well, the best reason we might decide not to carry it overseas is that most of the world—even including most of Western Europe—has a strong preference for the deductive approach.

Besides the United States, inductive is *in* only in England, Canada, Australia, Holland, Denmark, Sweden and Norway. In other words, it seems to be a markedly Anglo-Saxon characteristic. All of the rest of the world prefers the deductive approach! That's about 180 countries to 8! That's less than 4.5 percent who prefer the inductive approach!

Purpose of Education

A similar dichotomy would occur if we were to ask the people of any given country, *What is the purpose of education?* Numerically, the worldwide split would be in favor of those who feel the purpose should be to put factual information into students' heads. Of course, as American trainers and HRD specialists, we know the *right* answer is to help people *learn how to learn*. We feel learning how to learn is so much more worthwhile to do because that approach provides the person with a skill which will last a lifetime and because it enables people to learn *on their own*.

---

[7]Reginald Smart, in "Using a Western Learning Model in Asia: A Case Study," AFS Occasional Paper Number 4, June 1963.

In the following chart, I have transposed Bloom's Taxonomy[8] onto the familiar format of Maslow's Hierarchy.

Those who support Bloom's Taxonomy would argue that it has universal application. In fact it does *not*. Most students—from first grade in elementary school through the Ph.D. degree—around the world never go beyond the second level in Bloom's Taxonomy, and most of their activity remains on the first level. By contrast, by the time American students are in the sixth grade of elementary school, they are already working well into the fourth and fifth levels.

Adult foreigners are not dumb. They have simply never had the experience of applying factual data in the multiple ways we Americans do every day of our lives. And you can't take people who are comfortable only with the first level and barely conversant with the second level, and suddenly throw them into the fifth or sixth level and expect then to survive in it. This is what the American trainer who carries his inductive training program to the foreign setting is attempting to do.

The chart which appears on the next page is intended to be read from the bottom up. In other words, level 1 must be mastered before moving on to level 2, and so forth.

Moving a Deductive Learner into the Inductive Mode

In many instances it may indeed be desirable to consciously move a deductively oriented group into an inductive learning node. The inductive approach would be much more likely to develop creativity, for example, to offer one good reason for such a shift. Or if you wanted to develop any of the specific *higher level* skills on Bloom's chart, you would be much more likely to achieve this through inductive rather than deductive methodologies. Perhaps the best reason to move foreign-born students into this inductive mode would be to prepare them to study at an American university.

Such a shift cannot be accomplished overnight, however. Throwing a deductively oriented trainee from an Asian country into a role play, expecting him or her to assume an argumentative or assertive role two days after arrival in the U.S. is the surest way I know to put that person into a catatonic state.

I will suggest two ways to make the transition from deductive to inductive when, for valid reasons, it is consciously decided to do so.

Models for Change

The approaches I have personally found to work well in moving trainers from the deductive to the inductive mode are what I might refer to as a Progression Model and an Adaptation Model.

---

[8]Benjamin S. Bloom et al. (1956). *Taxonomy of educational objectives (Handbook I: Cognitive domain)*. New York: McKay. p. 18.

Hierarchy of Learning Skills

Λ

6. EVALUATION

Making qualitative and quantitative judgments about
the value of methods and materials for specified
purposes, applying a uniform standard. with
accuracy, consistency and objectivity.

5. SYNTHESIS

The putting together of elements to form a coherent whole
where none existed previously, whether a written document or
a plan of operation, plus the ability to formulate hypotheses
and generalizations from the newly organized materials.

4. ANALYSIS

Ability to break down communication into its constituent elements,
taking into account the relative importance of each part, whether the
material is elicit or implicit. thus recognizing unstated assumptions,
relationships. and organizing principles.

3. APPLICATION

Ability to turn abstractions into particular and concrete examples, whether
working with ideas, rules, theories, or generalized methods, plus the ability
to predict the effect of changes in component factors.

2. COMPREHENSION

Lowest level of understanding: the person is able to demonstrate he/she knows
what is being communicated by paraphrasing, interpreting (to any level of
generality), or extrapolating for consequences, corollaries, or effects.

1. KNOWLEDGE

Recall of factual data, in part or in whole: terminologies, facts and figures,
classification into categories, sequences, criteria, methodologies universals,
abstractions. principles, generalizations, and theories.

L. Robert Kohls, Meridian House International 1984
Adapted from Bloom et al

The Progression Model

Over a period of time, the facilitator can move, in a planned and systematic manner, from the most didactic to more experiential, more involving and even more *threatening* approaches.

The succession of methodologies succession I have found to work well is the following:

1. Lectures
↓
2. Lectures followed by Question and Answer Sessions
↓
3. Whole-Group Discussions
↓
4. Small Group Discussions (with groups of four[9]) and Reporting Back to the Full Session
↓
5. Discussion Based on Agree-Disagree Statements (with small groups assigned the task of coming to consensus)
↓
6. Case Studies (emphasizing multiple acceptable solutions rather than one "right" one)
↓
7. Single-Solution (programmed) Case Studies
↓
8. Role Plays (starting with non-threatening scenarios and moving to increasingly more threatening ones)

The movement, as can be seen, is from *cool* to *warm* activities. I would personally not attempt to move a deductively oriented group into even non-threatening role plays in less than three weeks of daily or near-daily contact (to give you some idea of the time involved)—so we are obviously not talking about a three-day workshop.

The Adaptation Model

I shall explain the Adaptation Model by example.

Several years ago, Reza Arasteh and I conceived the idea of developing a management training institution, in this country, which would accept only Third World and/or non-Western students and which would offer a two-year master's level program. The first

---

[9]The reason for using groups of four is that it is practically impossible for one member in that small a group to remain silent and unparticipative throughout the exercise. The other members will coax and urge the silent member to enter in with his/her ideas.

nine months would present Harvard-type management courses, exactly like those offered to American business majors (filled with such topics as decision making, time management, planning strategies, etc.). The summer would be spent working as management apprentices in American companies. During the first semester of the second year, the students would work in independent teams of two or three, with their own countrymen, to adapt all that they had learned to fit the management needs of their own country. The final semester of their second year, they would return home to field-test and modify their planned courses and exercises, with all of their adaptations.

As indicated, this plan is only an unimplemented idea in two dreamers' heads, but I am convinced that it, or some variation on it, would work very well.

Another way to adapt the American model to the needs of a particular country would be to identify an American who has several years' experience of living in the target country, and who has very positive attitudes toward that country and its people, and have him/her work with the trainer in redesigning the American course so as to adapt it to fit the target country's unique needs and expectations.

In both of these cases, there resides in a single person the knowledge and experience of two cultures: the American culture where the training was conceived, and the target country where the training is to be delivered. That bicultural person provides the mechanism to tie the two cultures together.

Conclusion

In the few pages of this paper I have touched on several issues which are relevant to our overall topic. Among the sub-topics are such issues as:

1. Ethnocentrism (each group's belief in the inherent superiority of its own culture);

2. The question of the appropriateness of one culture's approach in serving a different culture's needs;

3. The differences between inductive and deductive, or didactic and experiential, approaches (and what a tiny portion of the world—8/180ths or about 4.5 percent—prefers the inductive approach);

4. The purpose and applications of learning, and finally;

5. Some non-threatening ways, if we feel there is good reason to do so, of introducing a previously didactically and deductively inclined group to inductive and experiential learning techniques.

PHILOSOPHY
of
TRAINING

SECTION TITLES

ASSUMPTIONS WHICH UNDERLIE THE TRAINING ROLE

PHILOSOPHY OF TRAINING

SOME PRINCIPLES OF ADULT LEARNING

CREATING THE CLIMATE FOR LEARNING

ANDRAGOGY VS. PEDAGOGY

THE ASSUMPTIONS AND PROCESS ELEMENTS OF THE PEDAGOGICAL AND ANDRAGOGICAL MODELS OF LEARNING

CHARACTERISTICS OF ADULT LEARNERS

A GOOD TRAINER

ASSUMPTIONS WHICH UNDERLIE THE TRAINING ROLE

Frederic H. Margolis

1. Every individual has worth as a person. An individual is entitled to maintain his self-respect and dignity. His feelings are important and should be respected. Criticizing an individual's behavior is differentiated from rejecting him as a person.

2. Human beings have a capacity to learn and grow. Generally people do what they have learned to do and they usually follow the habits which have guided them in the past. Thus, they tend to be consistent in their actions. However, they also change their attitudes and beliefs and develop new ways of doing things as a result of new emotional-intellectual experiences.

3. The most effective type of learning—that which is most likely to influence attitudes and behavior—comes through having emotionally involving experiences and reflecting upon them. Individuals learn as they are stimulated and challenged to learn. They develop ways of behaving as they get responses (feedback) from other persons to their behavior.

4. A permissive atmosphere—a group climate conducive to free discussion and experimentation with different ways of behaving—is a necessary condition for learning. Only when an individual feels safe enough to behave as he normally does is it possible to detect the behaviors which are unproductive, i.e., those which are not effective with other persons. In a non-judgmental atmosphere a trainee is more likely to be receptive to feedback from others and willing to try different ways of expressing himself.

5. The training role carries responsibility for helping the trainees learn from their experiences. This involves facilitating the development of conditions within the group which will be conducive to learning and guiding the learning experience. It implies that the trainer as a person influences events within the group and that his behavior is also a legitimate subject for examination. In fact, the trainer's willingness to encourage scrutiny of his own role behavior is a crucial factor in furthering the growth of a climate which permits examination of the role behavior of members of the group.

6. The most productive way to work is to share the diagnosis of problems and to collaboratively plan and evaluate activities. This method leads to greater emotional involvement on the part of participants. It results in greater member commitment to decisions.

7. The study of *group process*, i.e., how work is done and the characteristics of the interaction among persons as they work, helps to improve group efficiency and productivity. The crucial factors which interfere with cooperative effort more often lie in the manner in which people work together than in the mastery of technical skills. Problems—of involvement, cooperative effort, of relationships between individuals, and of relations between individuals and the group—all are of universal nature. The best place to study such problems is in the immediate present. Hence, examination of what is going on in the group, the *here-and-now*, provides the richest material for learning. Every member can participate meaningfully because he has witnessed and experienced the data being discussed.

Source: Adapted from Frederic H. Margolis. (1970). *Training by objectives: a participant-oriented approach*, for Sterling Institute. Prepared for the Office of Economic Opportunity, June 1970.

PHILOSOPHY OF TRAINING

Richard L. Hopkins

1. Good training must be planned and managed; it doesn't just happen. Ad hoc training is never the most effective training possible.

2. Training represents a technology. The trainer has an understanding of how adults learn and he has a knowledge of, and an ability to draw upon a large variety of, appropriate training techniques and exercises. He knows which are most effective in training designed to:

   - increase or update knowledge,
   - develop skills, or
   - modify attitudes.

   A trainer doesn't have to be an expert in every field or discipline; he relies on content experts for this. The trainer's expertise is training.

3. Training should cause a change. Good training does make a difference.

4. Those changes should be specified beforehand, in learning objectives

5. Whenever possible, the learners should have an input in planning their own training.

6. Training should be action-oriented and involving. This forces relevance and makes the learning meaningful.

7. To the extent possible, training should be individualized, because everyone learns in different ways and because entry-level skills and competencies vary widely.

8. Trainers should function as facilitators, coaches, consultants, guides, and stimulators.

SOME PRINCIPLES OF ADULT LEARNING

Russell D. Robinson
(Adapted from Coolie Verner)

1. Learning is an active process and adults prefer to participate actively.

   - Therefore, those techniques that make provision for active participation will achieve more learning faster than those that do not.

2. Learning is goal directed, and adults are trying to achieve a goal or satisfy a need.

   - Therefore, the clearer, the more realistic and relevant the statement of the desired outcomes, the more learning that will take place.

3. Group learning, insofar as it creates a *learning atmosphere* of mutual support, may be more effective than individual learning.

   - Therefore, those techniques based on group participation are often more effective than those which handle individuals as isolated units.

4. Learning that is applied immediately is retained longer and is more subject to immediate use than that which is not.

   - Therefore, techniques must be employed that encourage the immediate application of any material in a practical way.

5. Learning must be reinforced.

   - Therefore, techniques must be used that insure prompt, reinforcing feedback.

6. Learning new material is facilitated when it is related to what is already known.

   - Therefore, the techniques used should help the adult establish this relationship and integration of material.

7. The existence of periodic plateaus in the rate of learning necessitates frequent changes in the nature of the learning task to insure continuous progress.

   - Therefore, techniques should be changed frequently in any given session.

8. Learning is facilitated when the learner is aware of his progress.

   - Therefore, techniques should be used that provide opportunities for self-appraisal.

9. Learning is facilitated when there is a logic to the subject matter and the logic makes sense in relation to the learner's repertoire of experience.

   - Therefore, learning must be organized for sequence and cumulative effects.

Source: Russell D. Robinson. (1979). *An introduction to helping adults learn and change.* (Revised 1994). West Bend, WI: Omnibook Company.

CREATING THE CLIMATE FOR LEARNING
Russell D. Robinson
(Adapted from Robert F. Mager)

Purpose of all instruction: the intent to send students away from instruction with at least as favorable an attitude toward the subject taught as they had when they first arrived.

People learn to avoid things they are hit with. If conditions for learning are unpleasant, people will avoid the situation, avoid learning, and may learn to hate the subject.

Need is to accentuate positive conditions and consequences in the learning situation and eliminate the negative, aversive conditions and consequences.

Aversive conditions to be eliminated:

1. Conditions which cause students fear and anxiety, distress, tension, foreboding, worry or disquiet, anticipation of the unpleasant.

2. Conditions which cause frustration, blocking, or interference with student's desire to learn.

3. Conditions which cause humiliation and embarrassment, causing lowering of a student's self-respect and self-esteem, making him uncomfortable or self-conscious or shaming, debasing or degrading him/her.

4. Conditions which cause boredom.

Positive conditions which create a climate for learning:

1. Acknowledging students' responses, whether correct or incorrect, as attempts to learn and following them with accepting rather than rejecting comments.

2. Providing instruction in increments that will allow success most of the time.

3. Providing enough sign posts so that the student always knows where he is and where he is expected to go.

4. Giving the student some choice in selecting and sequencing the subject matter.

5. Relating new information to old, within the experience of the student.

6. Treating the student as a person.

7. Providing instructional tasks that are relevant to your objectives and letting your student know what the objectives are.

Source: Russell D. Robinson. (1979). *An introduction to helping adults learn and change.* (Revised 1994). West Bend, WI: Omnibook Company.

ANDRAGOGY VS. PEDAGOGY

Russell D. Robinson

1. "Andragogy" is a word coined by Malcolm Knowles from the Greek word *aner* (with the stem *andr-*) meaning "man" and means "the art and science of helping adults learn" as distinguished from "pedagogy" (from the Greek stem *paid*— meaning child) which is the art and science of teaching children.

2. The Andragogical Process
   - The establishment of a climate conducive to adult learning.
   - The creation of an organizational structure for participative planning.
   - The diagnosis of needs for learning.
   - The formulation of directions of learning (objectives).
   - The development of a design of learning activities (plan).
   - The operation of the learning activities (implementation).
   - The rediagnosis of needs for learning (evaluation).

3. A comparison of andragogy and pedagogy:

ELEMENTS	PEDAGOGICAL Teacher Directed Learning	ANDRAGOGICAL Self-Directed Learning
Climate	Formal authority-oriented Competitive Judgmental	Informal, mutually respectful Consensual Collaborative Supportive
Planning	Primarily by teacher	By participative decision-making
Diagnosis of Needs	Primarily by teacher	By mutual assessment
Setting Goals	Primarily by teacher	By mutual negotiation
Designing a Learning Plan	Content units Course syllabus Logical sequence	Learning projects Learning content sequenced in terms of readiness
Learning Activities	Transmit techniques Assigned readings	Inquiry projects, independent study, experimental techniques
Evaluation	Primarily by teacher	By mutual assessment of self-collected evidence

Source: Russell D. Robinson. (1979). *An introduction to helping adults learn and change.* (Revised 1994). West Bend, WI: Omnibook Company.

THE ASSUMPTIONS AND PROCESS ELEMENTS OF THE PEDAGOGICAL AND ANDRAGOGICAL MODELS OF LEARNING

© 1980 Malcolm S. Knowles

ASSUMPTIONS

ABOUT	PEDAGOGICAL	ANDRAGOGICAL
Concept of the learner	Dependent personality	Increasingly self-directing
Role of learner's experience	Role of learner's experience	A rich source for learning by self and others
Readiness to learn	Uniform by age level and curriculum	Develops from life tasks and problems
Orientation to learning	Subject-centered	Task or problem centered
Motivation	By external rewards and punishment	By internal incentives, curiosity

PROCESS ELEMENTS

ELEMENTS	PEDAGOGICAL	ANDRAGOGICAL
Climate	Tense, low trust Formal, cold, aloof Authority-oriented Competitive Judgmental	Relaxed, trusting Mutually respectful Informal, warm Collaborative Supportive
Planning	Primarily by teacher	Mutually by learners and facilitator
Diagnosis of needs	Primarily by teacher	By mutual negotiation
Setting of objectives	Primarily by teacher	By mutual negotiation
Designing learning plans	Teacher's content plans Course syllabus Logical sequence	Learning contracts Learning projects Sequenced by readiness
Learning activities	Transmittal techniques Assigned readings	Inquiry projects Independent study Experiential techniques
Evaluation	By teacher Norm-referenced (on a curve) With grades	By learner-collected evidence validated by peers, facilitators and experts. Criterion referenced.

The body of theory and practice on which teacher-directed learning is based is often given the label *pedagogy*, from the Greek words *paid* (meaning child) and *agogus* (meaning guide or leader)—thus being defined as the art and science of teaching children.

The body of theory and practice on which self-directed learning is based is coming to be labeled *andragogy*, from the Greek word *aner*, (meaning adult)—thus being defined as the art and science of helping adults (or, even better, maturing human beings) learn.

These two models do not represent bad/good or child/adult dichotomies, but rather a continuum of assumptions to be checked out in terms of their rightness for particular learners in particular situations. If a pedagogical assumption is realistic for a particular situation, then pedagogical strategies are appropriate. For example, if a learner is entering into a totally strange content area, he or she will be dependent on a teacher until enough content has been acquired to enable self-directed inquiry to begin.

CHARACTERISTICS OF ADULT LEARNERS

Clive C. Veri and T.A. Vonder Haar

Adults must want to learn. This is the prime ingredient to an effective learning process. Much of the effort of the trainer should be to instill an appreciation for and a recognition of the constant need for upgrading knowledge and skills. The trainer helps the adult perceive a definite need for training.

Adults respond best to teaching/learning processes that involve active participation. To the extent real life situations can be simulated, the prospects of success increase. Most adults are impatient with abstractions.

The most effective and candid response to a teaching/learning situation will occur in an informal atmosphere. If the structure is too rigid, adults are not likely to penetrate the facade with embarrassing questions or alternate points of view. Informality encourages a livelier exchange of ideas and reduces normal tensions.

Adults progress most rapidly in learning situations that involve dealing with realistic problems. They appreciate solutions to their day-to-day concerns. They look for measurable benefits from the learning process.

Adults maintain interest by using a variety of methods. One single method, such as a lecture, can get monotonous.

Adults require reinforcement at each step. They neither care to invest effort if they are not confident they are moving in the right direction, nor want to commit resources such as time, energy and enthusiasm, only to find that they are misplaced. Reinforcement provides constant assurance that they are on the right track. Feedback is instantaneous evaluation of their efforts. When they are recognized as being on the right track, their sense of accomplishment spurs them on to new things. Feedback also provides the information when they are not on the right track, so the adult learner can quickly attempt to rectify the situation.

Ambiguity has no place in the learning process, especially as far as adults are concerned. They are apt to respond better when they know exactly what is expected of them in advance. Being particularly sensitive about mistakes and false directions, adults tend to move cautiously only after they know they have reasonable prospects for success. To lay out the whole program in the beginning of the training process will serve to reduce tension and increase the prospect for enthusiastic response.

Adults should be permitted to practice new skills. They want to put their motor abilities to work. But, as they attempt new efforts, it is important that they not become spectacles when mistakes are made. Learners, especially adults, should be made to realize that mistakes are expected, and that mistakes are important to the learning process. They must be assured that mistakes will be accepted without threat.

Source: Clive C. Veri and T. A. Vonder Haar. (1970). *Training the trainer*. St. Louis, MO: University of Missouri, Extension Division.

A Good Trainer

L. Robert Kohls

1. Doesn't dominate or impose. Lets trainees take the lead. Guides and facilitates rather than *directing* or *leading*.
    - Seems to have an overall *game plan*.
    - Senses when something isn't working and tries another approach.
    - Senses mood of the trainees and can change his/her game plan in mid-play, switching to something more appropriate than what he/she had planned.

2. Has knowledge of (and knows when to use) a large variety of training methods and techniques.
    - Chooses appropriate activities for each learning objective.
    - Is equally skillful in handling various techniques. Uses a good mix of techniques each day of the training program. Makes a smooth transition from one technique to the next.

3. Uses appropriate language. His/her explanations are understandable and succinct. Explains things in more than one way.

4. Senses the mood, spirit, and needs of the group.
    - Can laugh at himself/herself.
    - Can take a humorous comment and turn it to the advantage of training.
    - Asks for suggestions—and then takes those suggestions and acts on them.
    - Takes periodic *readings* of the group.
    - Seems to be in control at all times.

5. Announces the objectives for each session beforehand.
    - Doesn't lecture for long periods.
    - Generally uses more than one technique per session.
    - Usually chooses activities which fully involve the participants.
    - Discusses the trainees' reaction to the session afterwards. *Processes* every session.

6. Makes the trainees as aware of the process as the content.
    - Uses effective *group* methods. Gets all members of the group to contribute.
    - Distributes pertinent and worthwhile handouts (to reinforce learning).
    - Brings in community resource people.
    - Takes training out into the community when appropriate.

7. Tries to provide a lively setting for training (with posters, etc.) i.e., dresses up the training site.
    - Knows when to throw in an unscheduled break or a more active exercise for a change of pace.
    - Suggests there might be more than one possible answer to many problems.
    - Is willing to try out (e.g., in role play situation) various solutions suggested by the trainees.

8. Has faith that the trainees can arrive at workable solutions if given opportunity and chance.

- Has an ego that is not easily wounded.
- Can admit a mistake or that he/she doesn't know the answer to a question.
- If doesn't know, checks the information and returns with the correct answer later.

9. Is able to gain credibility quickly in a new group. Has a natural charisma. Is sincere; means what he/she says. Doesn't *play games* with the trainees.

- Seems to be training from a rich breadth of personal experience and concern for people. Gives impression he knows what he is talking about.
- Is Fair. Doesn't expect the trainees to go through anything he/she hasn't or wouldn't go through. Often joins in the group himself as one of the participants.

10. Generally keeps the attention of all the trainees when he/she is explaining the next activity.

- Is willing to give a straight answer to questions the trainees ask—even to questions of a personal nature.
- Joins in informal conversation with trainees during breaks. Usually with the trainees rather than with other staff members.

THE
TECHNOLOGY
of
TRAINING
(Instructional Systems Design)

SECTION TITLES

STEPS IN TRAINING DEVELOPMENT
THE TRAINING PROCESS
COURSE DEVELOPMENT
TIMETABLE FOR PLANNING
DESIGN CONSIDERATIONS

Steps in Training Development
L. Robert Kohls

Analysis:
Needs Assessment

Job Analysis/Job Description

Task Inventory

Performance Standards

Survey of Existing Courses

Learning Requirements Analysis

Site Selection

Design and Development
Overall Training Model

Course Content (Specification of Units and Content of Each Unit)

Performance Objectives

Determination of Sequence of Units and Time Allotment

Training Packages: Learning Activities, Media and Techniques, Handouts, Trainer(s) and Resource People, Sequence, Time Allotment, etc.

Evaluation design

Facilities and Scheduling

Materials Development: Training Manuals, Handouts, Tests

Training of Trainers

Materials Validation and Revision

Implementation:
Installation of Training Management System

Presentation of Individual Units

Evaluation:
Self-Evaluation

Internal Evaluation

External Evaluation

Feedback-Iteration Loop/Program Revision

THE TRAINING PROCESS

©1970 Clive C. Veri and T. A. Vonder Haar

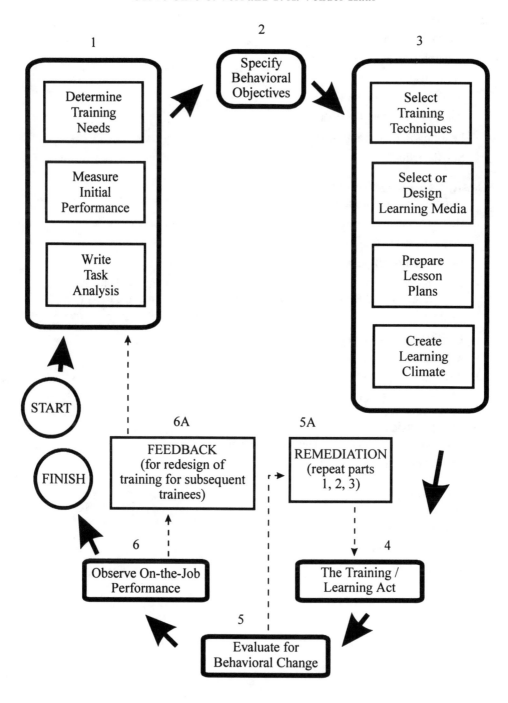

Source: Clive C. Veri and T. A. Vonder Haar. (1970). *Training the trainer*. St. Louis, MO: University of Missouri, Extension Division.

COURSE DEVELOPMENT

Russell D. Robinson

1. There are three phases in course development:

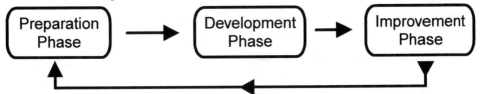

2. The preparation phase (needs, goals, objectives).
    *   Assessing Adult Needs
    *   Designing the Adult Learning Experience
    *   Developing Instructional Objectives
3. The development phase (developing the teaching plan) includes the following components:

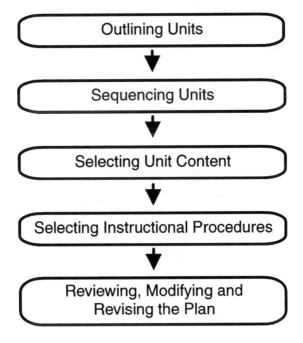

   As the arrow in the top chart indicates, the process then cycles back and keeps repeating itself as iteration after iteration of training occurs.

Source: Russell D. Robinson. (1979). *An introduction to helping adults learn and change*. (Revised 1994). West Bend, WI: Omnibook Company.

TIMETABLE FOR PLANNING
Russell D. Robinson

1. Several months ahead
- Determine audience, needs, focus, goals, methods
- List subjects; develop theme/title
- Determine price; estimate budget
- Select coordinator
- Determine location, dates

2. A few months ahead
- Prepare subjects and resource person lists
- Invite resource persons
- Determine and order mailing lists
- Draft publicity plans; prepare first press release
- Design brochure; prepare copy

3. Several weeks ahead
- Mail brochures
- Send out more press releases
- Order or prepare workbooks, other materials
- Determine time schedules of resource persons
- Make A/V requests
- Contact on-site personnel
- Establish registration procedures

4. A couple of weeks ahead
- Follow up on publicity
- Check on all on-site arrangements
- Send welcome letters to participants
- Reconfirm resource persons and time schedules

5. After the event
- Prepare final participant list
- Correspond with resource persons
- Review evaluation critiques

Source: Russell D. Robinson. (1979). *An introduction to helping adults learn and change.* (Revised 1994). West Bend, WI: Omnibook Company.

DESIGN CONSIDERATIONS

Russell D. Robinson

Change Desired	Some Basic Design Considerations
Knowledge	1. Specify key information. 2. Associate new information with learner's previous knowledge. 3. Help learners review and put information in own words.
Skills	1. Specify clearly skill goals (what, how, when, where, to what degree). 2. Help learners develop, practice ability levels. 3. Provide examples, models.
Attitudes	1. Help learners clarify values, discuss points of view. 2. Emphasize advantages, positives. 3. Help learners empathize with views discrepant to their own. 4. Provide channels for continuing support over long-term.
Creativity	1. Help learner develop a creative mental set. 2. List and record creative ideas. 3. Reward creativity.

Source: Russell D. Robinson. (1979). *An introduction to helping adults learn and change.* (Revised 1994). West Bend, WI: Omnibook Company.

NEEDS
ASSESSMENT AND / OR
TASK ANALYSIS

SECTION TITLES

NEEDS ASSESSMENT METHODS
NINE BASIC NEEDS ASSESSMENT METHODS
TASK ANALYSIS

NEEDS ASSESSMENT METHODS

Russell D. Robinson

1. Individual Assessment

- Though adults in learning settings are accustomed to having their learning needs decided for them, once they experience the process of assessing their own needs, they prefer this to having someone else decide.

- The process involves learners in building their own competency models for self-development and then comparing their present situations against the models.

2. Group (Assessment) Discussion

- Assessing learning needs in small groups in which members help each other to clarify their individual needs enables them to become resources for each other's learning.

- The process may involve collecting group discussion data on newsprint and hanging up the list for all to see so they can *keep track* of their discussion.

3. Questionnaires and Surveys

- Data gathering devices such as check lists, sentence completion, questionnaires, or organizational or community surveys, may be relatively simple or quite sophisticated.

- In any case, such devices should be pre-tested, revised to avoid bias, and administered to preserve anonymity.

- It is important that findings be reported to the population surveyed and that the needs generated be responded to.

4. Systems Analysis

- Methods of systems analysis, or input/output analysis, may be used to analyze organizations as functioning social systems according to systems criteria such as feedback flow, input/output relationship, and the relationship of systems and subsystems.

5. Organizational or Community Records and Reports

- Operating records can often indicate trends or give clues to the existence of potential learning needs.

- Needs are often made apparent as a result of formal studies or research activities conducted by organizations.

6. Professional Literature

- Often professional journals or articles raise questions or produce new insights that lead directly to an increased awareness of learning needs. A review of professional literature can help identify needs in special fields or activities.

Source: Russell D. Robinson. (1979). *An introduction to helping adults learn and change*. (Revised 1994). West Bend, WI: Omnibook Company.

7. Resource Persons

- Talking to experts in various activities can help gather additional information or gain a different perspective about learning needs.

8. Tests

- Diagnostic tools may he used to identify specific areas of deficiencies.

- Tests may be threatening to adults. A climate needs to be established for the test.

- Tests, obviously, must be appropriate. Some tests may not measure what they are supposed to measure and results would have little value.

9. Analysis and Performance Review

- A job analysis provides specific and precise information about jobs and performance.

- It is time-consuming and difficult to do by people not specifically trained in job analysis techniques.

- Analysis, obviously, must be of current job and current performance.

NINE BASIC NEEDS ASSESSMENT METHODS

Stephen V. Steadham

Methods	Advantages	Disadvantages
1. Observation • Can be as technical as time-motion studies or as functionally or behaviorally specific as observing a new board or staff member interacting during a meeting. • May be as unstructured as walking through an agency's offices on the lookout for evidence of communications barriers. • Can be used normatively to distinguish between effective and ineffective behaviors, organizational structures and/or processes.	• Minimizes interruption of routine work flow or group activity. • Generates *in situ* data, highly relevant to the situation where response to identified training needs/interests will impact. • (When combining with a feedback step) provides for important comparison checks between inferences of the observer and respondent.	• Requires a highly skilled observer with both process and content knowledge (unlike an interviewer who needs, for the most part, only process skill). • Carries limitations that derive from being able to collect data only within the work setting (the other side of the first advantage listed in the preceding column). • Holds potential for respondents to perceive the observation activity as spying.
2. Questionnaires • May be in the form of surveys or polls of a random or stratified sample of respondents or, an enumeration of an entire population. • Can use a variety of question formats, open-ended, projective, forced choice, priority ranking. • Can take alternative forms such as Q-sorts, or slip sorts, rating scales, either pre-designed or self-generated by respondent(s). • May be self administered (by mail) under controlled or uncontrolled conditions, or may require the presence of an interpreter or assistant.	• Can reach a large number of people in a short time. • Are relatively inexpensive. • Give opportunity of expression without fear of embarrassment. • Yield data easily summarized and reported.	• Make little provision for free expression of unanticipated responses. • Require substantial time (and technical skills, especially in survey mode) for development of effective instruments. • Are of limited utility in getting at the causes of problems or possible solutions. • Suffer low return rates (mailed), grudging responses, or unintended and/or inappropriate respondents.

Source: Stephen V. Steadham. (1980). "Learning to Select a Needs Assessment Strategy." *Training and Development Journal.* ASTD, January 1980.

Methods	Advantages	Disadvantages

3. Key Consultation
 	
• Secures information from those persons, who by virtue of their formal standing, are in a good position to know what the training needs of a particular group are:
 	
  a. board chairman
  b. related service providers
  c. members of professional associations
  d. individuals from the service populations.
 	
• Once identified, data can be gathered from these consultants by using techniques such as interviews, group discussions, questionnaires.
	• Is relatively simple and inexpensive to conduct.
	
	• Permits input and interaction of a number of individuals, each with his or her own perspectives of the needs of the area, discipline, group, etc.
	
	• Establishes and strengthens lines of communication between participants in the process.
		• Carries a built-in bias, since it is based on views of those who tend to see training needs from their own individual or organizational perspective.
		
		• May result in only a partial picture of training needs due to the typically non-representative nature (in a statistical sense) of a key informant group.

4. Print Media • Can include professional journals, legislative news/notes, industry *rags*, trade magazines, in-house publications.	• Is an excellent source of information for uncovering and clarifying normative needs. • Provides information that is current, is not forward-looking. • Is readily available and is apt to have already been reviewed by the client group.	• Can be a problem when it comes to the data analysis and synthesis into a usable form (use of clipping service or key consultants can make this kind of data more usable).

Methods	Advantages	Disadvantages
5. Interviews • Can be formal or casual, structured or unstructured, or somewhere in between. • May be used with a sample of a particular group (board, staff, committee), or conducted with everyone concerned. • Can be done in person, by phone, at the work site or away from it.	• Are adept at revealing feelings, causes of and possible solutions to problems which the client is facing (or anticipates), provide maximum opportunity for the client to represent himself spontaneously on his own terms (especially when conducted in an open-ended non-directive manner.	• Are usually time consuming. • Can be difficult to analyze and quantify results (especially from unstructured formats). • Unless the interviewer is skillful, the client(s) can easily be made to feel self-conscious. • Rely for success on a skillful interviewer who can generate data without making (clients) feel self-conscious, suspicious, etc.
6. Group Discussion • Resembles face-to-face interview technique, e.g. structured or unstructured formal or informal, or somewhere in between. • Can be focused on job (role) analysis, group problem analysis, group goal setting, or any number of group tasks or themes, e.g. leadership training needs of the board. • Uses one or several of the familiar group facilitating techniques: brainstorming, nominal group process, force-fields, consensus, rankings, organizational mirroring, simulation, and sculpting.	• Permits on-the-spot synthesis of different viewpoints. • Builds support for the particular service response that is ultimately decided on. • Decreases *client-dependent response* toward the service provider since data analysis is (or can be) a shared function. • Helps participants to become better problem analysts, better listeners, etc.	• Is time consuming (therefore initially expensive) both for the consultant and the agency. • Can produce data that are difficult to synthesize and quantify (more a problem with the less structured techniques).

Methods	Advantages	Disadvantages
7. Tests • Are a hybridized form of questionnaire. • Can be very functionally oriented (like observations) to test a board, staff, or committee member's proficiency. • May be used to sample learned ideas and facts. • Can be administered with or without the presence of an assistant.	• Can be especially helpful in determining whether the cause of a recognized problem is a deficiency in knowledge or skill or by elimination, attitude. • Results are easily quantifiable and comparable.	• The availability of a relatively small number of tests that are validated for a specific situation. • Do not indicate if measured knowledge and skills are actually being used in the *on-the-job* or *back home group* situation.
8. Records, Reports • Can consist of organizational charts, planning documents, policy manuals, audits and budget reports. • Employee records, (grievances, turnover, accidents, etc.). • Includes minutes of meetings, weekly/ monthly program reports, memoranda, agency service records, program evaluation studies.	• Provide excellent clues to trouble spots. • Provide objective evidence of the results of problems within the agency or group. • Can be collected with a minimum of effort and interruption of work flow since it already exists at the work site.	• Causes of problems or possible solutions often do not show up. • Carries perspective that generally reflects the past situation rather than the current one (or recent changes). • Need a skilled data analyst if clear patterns and trends are to emerge from such technical and diffuse raw data.
9. Work Samples • Are similar to Observation but in written form. • Can be products generated in the course of the organization's work, e.g. ad layouts, program proposals, market analyses, letters, training designs, or • Written responses to a hypothetical but relevant case. • Study provided by the consultant.	• Carry most of the advantages of records and reports data. • Are the organization's data (its own output).	• Case study methods will take time away from actual work of the organization. • Need specialized content analysis. • Analyst's assessment of strengths/weaknesses disclosed by samples can be challenged as too subjective.

TASK ANALYSIS

Clive C. Veri and T.A. Vonder Haar

The blueprint for training is the TASK ANALYSIS.

The TASK ANALYSIS Includes

- Job title
- Major tasks of the job
- Qualitative standards
- Quantitative aspects
- Skills and educational requirements
- Materials and instruments needed
- Time in which each sub-task is to be completed; deadlines
- Constraints anticipated and to be overcome
- Resources that can be summoned to deal with the constraints
- Preferred methodology
- Other considerations

The *Task Analysis* is not designed to box in an employee by depriving him/her of the flexibility that is essential in most jobs. If the employee is expected to exercise good judgment, there must be room for him/her to select alternatives. As society changes, institutional objectives change, so that a *Task Analysis* is fluid, subject to continuing revisions appropriate to the time.

The TASK ANALYSIS Provides

- Efficient measures of production
- Accurate indicators of training needs
- Instruments for forecasting future production and needs
- Sets of expectations for each employee
- Opportunities for the employee to think about the job
- Fair methods of evaluating performance
- Simple ways of documenting reports
- Handy devices for filling vacancies
- The elimination of *buck passing*
- The writing of institutional objectives

The TASK ANALYSIS Provides

Efficient measures of production. Since quantitative aspects of a given task are stated in the *Task Analysis*, the sum of several tasks indicates how much is being done.

Accurate indicators of training needs. Since the *Task Analysis* specifies the desired level of behavior for a given task, pre-testing can determine the gap between initial

---

Source: Clive C. Veri and T. A. Vonder Haar. (1970). *Training the trainer*. St. Louis, MO: University of Missouri, Extension Division.

proficiency and autonomy, thus precisely indicating training needs.

Instruments for forecasting future production and needs. A good *Task Analysis* cannot be drawn up unless particular attention is directed to present needs. From that point, it is but one step to think about future needs. Accumulated *Task Analyses* can provide clues to developmental changes, thus providing clues as to what changes can be expected in the future.

Sets of expectations for each employee. When the trainee or employee sees the whole task laid out in detail before him/her, he/she can prepare physically, mentally, and psychologically. Because he/she sees the entire picture, he/she can understand all the components of the task and thus carry out the operation more efficiently. There are no surprises. His/her familiarity with what is expected of him/her reduces tension and encourages compliance.

Opportunities for the employee to think about his/her job. If the employee is encouraged to sit down and think about a given task, he/she may, on the basis of his/her experience, offer suggestions as to how the task can be performed more efficiently, with fewer exertions of resources, or in less time. As the employee assembles all the components of the task, he/she feels responsible for its completion. Because he/she participates in the writing of the *Task Analysis*, he/she feels committed, particularly if he/she has agreed to all the aspects. If he/she feels the *Task Analysis* is the result of his/her effort, chances are he/she will perform the task according to all specifications with no supervision.

Fair methods of evaluating performance. Because all aspects of the *Task Analysis* are committed to writing previous to implementation, misunderstanding about the quality or quantity of work is unlikely. The evaluative criteria are established beforehand. Because of this, a trainee can evaluate himself accurately. In this case, involvement by the trainer is lessened. If the trainee can evaluate himself accurately, he/she can identify his/her own deficiencies. If he/she can identify his/her own deficiencies, he/she will be receptive to improving performance and appropriate training. Personal whims are removed from the evaluation process when the criteria are established beforehand in the *Task Analysis* system.

Simple ways of documenting reports. Just as the *Task Analysis* informs everyone what work will be performed in the future, it provides a measure of that which was done in the past. Reports that conform to the structure of the *Task Analysis* can be easily compiled.

Handy devices for filling vacancies. When a change in personnel takes place, recruiting is simplified because the recruiter knows exactly what to look for in a replacement. When the replacement arrives, he/she knows exactly how to fill the space because it is all specifically listed on the *Task Analysis* sheet.

The elimination of *buck-passing*. As each member of an agency writes his/her *Task Analysis*, the inevitable questions as to who performs what tasks cannot be avoided. Responsibility for certain decisions is clearly designated. Agencies oriented toward *Task Analysis* will not be able to procrastinate, or otherwise avoid making the tough decisions.

The writing of institutional objectives. If the heads of departments or agencies fail to communicate institutional objectives to all employees, there is little consistency of operation and much waste of resources. Occasionally, institutional objectives are not communicated because those responsible for the formulation of those objectives are unwilling or unable to make them. They prefer perhaps to work in an atmosphere of ambiguity and confusion in order not to be committed to a specific philosophy. If each individual within a given agency operates according to his/her own philosophy, he/she works at cross purposes with others in the agency, a wasteful situation at best. High morale is not likely to blossom in agencies where the manner and philosophy of serving the clientele is not clearly stated.

Without a comprehensive *Task Analysis* system, an organization may fail to be sensitive to the needs of the people the agency is supposed to serve. When this happens, energetic reactions by the clientele group may cause the serving agency to be even more afraid to make decisions, causing further deterioration of morale and efficiency, until finally the entire system breaks down.

Task Analysis is designed as a system to marshal all available resources in response to the people's needs.

After the first writing of the *Task Analysis*, the next step is establishing priorities. In the course of a given work period, what are those tasks that MUST be performed? All levels of administration throughout the organization should work together to agree on a system of priorities. Tasks should be listed in terms of importance.

Those employees who are chronically worried about constant invasion of their in-basket should be encouraged to sort out those tasks that can wait. If they learn to commit their efforts to the tasks of priority importance, they might learn that the less important things tend to take care of themselves.

Some employees love to be overburdened by work. Their in-baskets are piled high, perspiration beads on the forehead, looks of perpetual consternation and martyrdom fish out for sympathy. Some overworked employees like conveying the impression that many urgent items require their personal and immediate attention.

In some organizations, playing the role of work substitutes for work itself. The only reliable index of output is the constant flow of complaints and signs of frustration. The person who works according to a well-thought-out system of priorities conserves his/her physical, nervous and mental strength and other resources for the important things. He/she realizes that some aspects of his/her job are more important than others. He addresses himself to minor matters when he/she has the time.

Chances are the employee with these attitudes is happier, more reliable, more stable, and a more efficient producer.

DEVELOPING
BEHAVIORAL
OBJECTIVES

Section Titles

Behavioral Objectives
Behavioral Objectives Checklist
Aids In Developing Behavioral Objectives

BEHAVIORAL OBJECTIVES

Robert F. Mager

"If you're not sure where you're going, you're liable to end up someplace else."

Robert F. Mager

A Behavioral Objective

- Is measurable
- States the level of acceptable performance
- Specifies the conditions under which the trainee is to perform the tasks

Characteristics

- Performance (what the learner is able to do)
- Conditions (important conditions under which the performance is expected to occur)
- Criterion (the quality or level of performance that will be considered acceptable)

Example

Upon successful completion of the workshop, the trainee will be able, without using reference materials, to describe three common points of view regarding ethnic superiority or inferiority which are not supported by research.

Source: Robert F. Mager. (1975). *Preparing instructional objectives (a self-programmed workbook)*. Belmont, CA: Fearon Publishers, Inc.

BEHAVIORAL OBJECTIVES CHECKLIST

General Learning Corporation

Use the following questions to guide your analysis of an instructional objective to determine its level of acceptability. A *no* answer to any question will pinpoint a characteristic that is missing or ambiguously stated. Clarity is judged by whether or not another person's restatement of the objectives is consistent with your intent.

1. Is it clear WHO will be performing the action?

    It is not always necessary to state the "who" explicitly (the learner, the student, the trainee) unless there might be confusion about who is performing. Objectives should be written in terms of the learner's performance.

2. Is it clear WHAT the learner will be doing? Is the behavior observable and/or measurable?

3. Is it clear UNDER WHAT CONDITIONS the learner will be performing?

    There are two aspects to this characteristic:

    a. It may be appropriate to specify what the learner will be provided with or denied (a dictionary, a slide rule, forms, reference books) .

    b. It may be appropriate to describe the situation in which you expect the behavior to occur (when conducting a CAA board meeting...; when confronted by an irate citizen...; when preparing to submit a proposal; on a paper and pencil test...).

4. Is it clear WHAT LEVEL OF PROFICIENCY OR COMPETENCY is expected?

    This may be stated in such terms as a number of percentage of correct test items, a change in score on an attitude inventory, execution of a process according to prescribed sequence or other criteria. If time is a factor in successful performance, that may be specified as well.

5. Is it clear WHEN this behavior is expected to be demonstrated?

    This characteristic is usually stated in terms of the length of the instructional experience (at the end of a session, at the end of a week, after a certain number of practice sessions). As in item 1 above, an explicit statement is optional unless there is a chance of confusion.

AIDS IN DEVELOPING BEHAVIORAL OBJECTIVES

Benjamin S. Bloom and Others

Cognitive Domain

The *Taxonomy of Educational Objectives,* edited by Bloom, offers guidance to the classification of educational goals in the cognitive domain. This chart, which follows, was developed from Bloom's Handbook *Cognitive Domain,* and it can be used by the training specialist to identify learning levels and to decide on appropriate terms for stating objectives.

Psychomotor Domain

The *Classification of Educational Objectives,* by Simpson, offers guidance in the psychomotor domain. This chart, developed from Simpson's project report, can be used by training specialists to identify learning levels and to decide on appropriate terms for stating objectives.

Affective Domain

The *Taxonomy of Educational Objectives,* by Krathwohl, Bloom, and Masia, offers guidance to the classification of educational goals in the affective domain. This chart, developed from their *Handbook II,* can be used by the training specialist to identify major learning levels in this domain and to decide on appropriate terms for stating objectives.

Refer to charts on the following three pages.

Cognitive Domain[1]

Description of learning levels	Sample Task Statements	Terms used to identify cognitive behavior
Level 1.0 Knowledge. The learner's behavior ranges from the remembering of specific bits of information, i.e. terminology, to recall of universals and abstractions, i.e., theory.	• Matches machine parts and their names. • Outlines the five-step training procedure. • Knows the fundamentals of first-level supervision.	Defines, describes, identifies, labels, lists, names, reproduces, selects, states.
Level 2.0 Comprehension. The learner's behavior ranges from the translation of concepts, by paraphrasing, through interpretation, i.e. extrapolation.	• Interprets an engineering drawing. • Converts an illustrative DSM plan to the back-home action plan. • Generalizes a problem-solving technique to retail management practice.	Defends, distinguishes, estimates, explains, gives examples, infers, justifies, paraphrases, predicts, rewrites, summarizes, translates, understands.
Level 3.0 Application. The learner's behavior demonstrates the use of previous learning in new and concrete situations.	• Produces guidelines for establishing new employee policy. • Solves mail distribution. • Demonstrates window service selling techniques.	Applies, changes, computes, constructs, discovers, manipulates, modifies, operates, predicts, prepares, relates, shows, uses.
Level 4.0 Analysis. The learner's behavior shows ability to break information down into its elements, through an understanding of content and structure.	• Diagrams operational procedures. • Identifies personnel problems in work situations. • Recognizes deficiencies in mail routing schemes.	Analyzes, breaks down, differentiates, distinguishes, evaluates, illustrates, infers, outlines, points out, relates, selects, separates, subdivides.
Level 5.0 Synthesis. The learner's behavior shows ability to assemble elements and parts, to form new patterns or structures.	• Gives a well organized welcome speech. • Designs an LSM mechanical course. • Reorganizes office management procedures.	Categorizes, combines, compiles, composes, creates, devises, explains, formulates, generates, integrates, modifies, organizes, plans, rearranges, reconstructs, relates, revises, rewrites, summarizes, tells.
Level 6.0 Evaluation. The learner's behavior demonstrates ability to make judgments based on definite internal and external criteria. The learner may be given the criteria or develop his or her own criteria.	• Compares the cost-effectiveness of instructional materials. • Judges the street performance of motorized carriers training by use of department standards.	Appraises, concludes, contrasts, criticizes, describes, discriminates, explains, justifies, interprets, relates, summarizes, supports.

---

[1]Adapted from Benjamin S. Bloom, et al. (1956). *Taxonomy of Educational Objectives (Handbook I: Cognitive Domain)*. New York: McKay.

Psychomotor Domain[2]

Description of learning levels	Sample Task statements for psychomotor-type objectives	Terms used to identify psychomotor behavior
Level 1.0 Perception. The learner's behavior ranges from contact of a sense organ with a stimulus, through identification of a cue or cues associated with a task, and the mental process of determining the meaning of cues received for action.	• Feels belt tension. • Identifies engine noises. • Recognizes mail shapes and sizes.	Decides action, handles, hears, holds, identifies flavor, forms, sound or odor, observes, sees, smells, scans, tastes, touches.
Level 2.0 Set. The learner's behavior signifies completion of mental and emotional adjustments and readiness to perform a motor act.	• Reviews procedures mentally. • Acknowledges readiness for task by pulling on gloves, or nodding head to snap face shield down. • Readies himself/herself by reading checklist aloud.	Expresses (indicates) readiness or adjustment, establishes, orients, prepares.
Level 3.0 Guided response. The learner's behavior indicates attempts to develop components of a complex motor skill, either through imitation or trial and error.	• Handles tools and materials used in electric motor repair. • Drafts a freehand sketch of a machine part. • Tries to type 60 words per minute.	Attempts, develops, exercises, follows up, interprets directions, originates, practices.
Level 4.0 Mechanism. The learner's behavior shows some confidence and competence during the performance of a motor act and indicates acquisition of a learned response.	• Installs a bolt, washer, and nut. • Cases a ledge of letter mail. • Executes a foreign mail distribution scheme.	Accomplishes, arranges, demonstrates, effects, exhibits, handles, heaves, holds, implements, inserts, launches, lays out loads, mans, maneuvers, manipulates, marks, masks, packages, packs, patches, performs, places, poises, purges, releases, rigs, secures, sets up, shifts, splices, stacks, sterilizes, stores, tempers, tests, tows, traces, transfers, transports, trues, tunes, upends, vents, welds.
Level 5.0. Complex overt response. The learner's behavior demonstrates a smooth and efficient movement pattern when performing a motor act requiring multiple responses. The learner knows the sequence, proceeds with confidence, is at ease, and has muscle control.	• Aligns driver and driven couplings. • Assembles a lobby display. • Services stamp vending machines.	Adjusts, applies, breaks-out, carries out, charts, compensates, compounds, consolidates, corrects, demonstrates, disassembles, dresses, drives, effects, executes, fabricates, fits, grinds in, implements, inspects, machines, maintains, mans, measures, manipulates, operates, overhauls, sets up, synchronizes, takes action, troubleshoots.

[2]Adapted from Simpson. (1966). *The Classification of Educational Objectives, Psychomotor Domain*. Project Report, University of Illinois.

Affective Domain[3]

Descriptions of learning levels	Sample task statements for affective-type objectives	Terms used to identify affective behavior
Level 1.0 Receiving. The learner's behavior ranges from awareness that a learning experience is occurring to attention to specific details of lesson.	• Follows directions. • Identifies a need to study for back-home assignments. • Uses instructional materials.	Accepts, asks, attends, chooses, describes, gives, holds, listens, locates, names, points to, selects, shows awareness or sensitivity, sits erect, replies.
Level 2.0 Responding. The learner's behavior ranges from a willingness to react to the learning environment to an expression of interest in the subject.	• Discusses the subject with others. • Reads beyond the study assignment. • Answers questions with personal opinion.	Assists, completes, compiles, conforms, enjoys, greets, helps, labels, participates, performs, practices, presents, obeys, shows interest, volunteers.
Level 3.0 Valuing. The learner's behavior ranges from acceptance of the worth of a new behavior or phenomenon to a commitment involving support of a value. (Appreciation—and attitude—type objectives are at this level.)	• Joins a professional organization. • Appreciates good personal management. • Demonstrates commitment to the use of planning skills.	Completes, describes, demonstrates attitudes or belief, differentiates, explains, follows, forms, initiates, invites, justifies, proposes, reads, reports, selects, shares, studies, works.
Level 4.0 Organization. The learner's behavior ranges from the assimilation of different values to the formation of a new and consistent value system.	• Compares Theory X with Theory Y to develop a management philosophy. • Integrates human engineering principles into a machine design to improve operator health and safety.	Accepts, adheres, alters, arranges, combines, completes, defends, explains, formulates, generalizes, identifies, modifies, orders, prepares, recognizes, relates, synthesizes, understands.
Level 5.0 Characterization by value or value complex. The learner's behavior is typical and consistent with his or her entrenched value system.	• Influences peers by assuming leadership responsibilities. • Performs quality assurance assignments. • Maintains safe work station.	Acts, demonstrates, discriminates, displays, listens, modifies, performs, practices, proposes, qualifies, questions, revises, serves, solves, uses, verifies.

---

[3]Adapted from Benjamin S. Bloom, et al. (1950). *Taxonomy of Educational Objectives (Handbook II)*. New York: McKay.

TRAINER
COMPETENCIES
and
TRAINER
ROLES

SECTION TITLES

WHAT TO LOOK FOR IN AN INTERCULTURAL TRAINER
TRAINER COMPETENCIES FOR THE CROSS-CULTURAL TRAINER
COMPETENCIES IN THE TRAINING AND DEVELOPMENT MODEL
THE FIFTEEN KEY TRAINING AND DEVELOPMENT ROLES
MEASURING THE TRAINER'S EFFECTIVENESS
SELF-DIAGNOSTIC RATING SCALE: COMPETENCIES FOR THE ROLE OF ADULT EDUCATOR/TRAINER

WHAT TO LOOK FOR IN AN INTERCULTURAL TRAINER

L. Robert Kohls

1. Area Knowledge of the target country, gained either through first-hand experience or through study.

2. Living experience in the target country, of a minimum of two years (and preferably longer).

3. A positive attitude toward the country and toward the people of that country.

4. The experience of having lived through culture shock (somewhere).

5. A fundamental knowledge of basic American values and implicit assumptions and how to articulate them.

6. Experience as a trainer, especially as a stand-up trainer and, particularly, in processing a variety of experiential learning techniques.

7. Interest in training for content as well as process.

Source: L. Robert Kohls. (1984). *Intercultural training: don't leave home without it.* Washington, DC: SIETAR.

TRAINER COMPETENCIES FOR THE INTERCULTURAL TRAINER

R. Michael Paige

Trainer Competencies in the Cognitive Domain

Knowledge Area	Knowledge Specifics
Intercultural Phenomena	1. intercultural effectiveness, competence
	2. intercultural adjustment, culture shock
	3. reentry adjustment
	4. culture learning
	5. the psychological and social dynamics of the intercultural experience
Intercultural Training	6. training-program assumptions: program philosophy, conceptual foundations of training perspectives on learner needs, etc.
	7. program-planning principles: client-needs assessment, audience analysis, staff training, logistics, timing, length, setting
	8. key training variables: audience diversity, trainer skills, length of program, predicted intensity of the intercultural experience, amount of affective and behavioral training
	9. realistic understanding of what training can and cannot accomplish
	10. realistic understanding of the relationship of training to performance in the target culture
	11. training design: goals and objectives, appropriate use of experiential and didactic methods, culture-specific and culture-general content, cognitive/affective/behavioral learning, and integrated training designs which incorporate these elements
	12. training pedagogy: appropriate selection and sequencing of learning activities, alternative training techniques, purposes of different activities, techniques for preparing culture learners (learning how to learn)
	13. program evaluation principles and methods

Source: Paige, R. Michael, ed. (1993). *Education for the intercultural experience.* Reprinted with permission of Intercultural Press, Inc., Yarmouth, ME. Copyright, 1993.

Trainer-Learner Issues	14. debriefing principles and strategies
	15. the social-psychological dynamics of the trainer-learner relationship: power, role modeling, risk of learner dependence on trainer
	16. the nature and sources of learner resistance to training and potential learner reactions to intense training experiences (stress, anxiety, frustration, anger)
	17. major learner concerns: threat to cultural identity, pressures to assimilate, challenge of becoming multicultural, becoming immobilized in a state of cultural relativism
Ethical Issues	18. ethical issues in training: appropriate management of risks faced by learners (failure, self-disclosure), proper handling of the transformation imperative of training, creating a supportive rather than destructive learning environment
	19. the intercultural trainer's code of ethics
Culture-Specific Content	20. the target culture: political, economic, social, cultural, demographic, religious, historical, and other factors
	21. situational factors in the target culture: host-counterpart expectations, job clarity, openness to outsiders, host-culture/country relationship to own culture/country, host-culture country aspirations
	22. predominant values, attitudes, and behaviors in the host culture
	23. the nature of the occupational position: job roles and requirements
Trainer Issues	24. the role of the trainer in the learning process
	25. the pressures that face trainers and methods for coping with them
	26. one's own strengths and limitations as a trainer
International Issues	27. theories of development, social change, transfer of technology
	28. the issues of international relations: dependence versus interdependence, neocolonialism, parity versus dominance
Multicultural Issues	29. cultural pluralism and diversity: diversity and intercultural interactions in the workplace and in society
	30. the nature and impact of racism, sexism, and other forms of prejudice and discrimination; institutionalized forms of prejudice and discrimination
	31. history of oppression and discrimination of groups being trained; history of intergroup relations among groups being trained
	32. the psychology of cultural marginality and multiculturalism

Trainer Competencies in the Behavioral Domain

Behavioral Area	Specific Behavioral Capacities
Intercultural Phenomena	1. capacity to promote learner acquisition of skills, knowledge, and personal qualities relevant to intercultural effectiveness 2. capacity to induce a cultural-adjustment experience and to provide a culture-general conceptual framework to assist learners in coping with adjustment stresses 3. capacity to conceptualize reentry issues and provide concrete ways for learners to maintain their connectedness with their home culture 4. capacity to conceptualize the culture-learning phenomenon as a framework for thinking about intercultural experiences 5. capacity to present theories and concepts regarding the psychological and social dynamics of the intercultural experience: culture shock, intercultural communication and interaction, intercultural competence, etc.
Intercultural Training	6. ability to articulate a clear, theory- and research-based training philosophy and a statement of central training-program assumptions 7. ability to conduct planning activities, including staff training and development, needs analysis, audience assessment 8. ability to effectively consider key training variables in program planning, design, and pedagogy 9. ability to make appropriate claims for what training can and cannot accomplish 10. ability to make appropriate claims regarding the relationship of training to performance in the target culture 11. ability to design integrated training programs having the appropriate mix of experiential and didactic methods, culture-specific and culture-general content, cognitive/affective/behavioral-learning activities 12. ability to implement training pedagogy which effectively selects and sequences learning activities; utilizes alternative training techniques; clearly realizes the cognitive, affective, and behavioral purposes of different learning activities; and incorporates appropriate techniques for preparing culture learners (learning how to learn) 13. ability to conduct formative and summative program evaluations

Trainer-Learner Issues	14. ability to debrief learning activities with individuals and groups 15. capacity to establish effective relationships with learners which reduce risk of learner dependence, minimize power and status differentials, build trust in the learning community 16. capacity to help learners deal with stress, anxiety, frustration, etc.; ability to respond effectively and with sensitivity to learner resistance 17. capacity to effectively treat difficult issues—cultural identity, assimilation, multiculturalism, cultural relativism—in training design and pedagogy
Ethical Issues	18. capacity to incorporate ethical standards into all aspects of training 19. capacity to adhere firmly to the intercultural trainer's code of ethics, the ethical guidelines of the profession; this includes the willingness to improve one's own professional skills
Culture-Specific Content	20. capacity to secure appropriate information about and resources on the target culture: values, attitudes, politics, history, geography, etc. 21. capacity to assess situational factors in the field that will affect the work of the sojourner 22. ability to assess and describe specific job roles, duties, and host-counterpart expectations 23. ability to provide instruction regarding target culture
Trainer Issues	24. capacity to articulate, model, and orient learners to a clear philosophy of the trainer's role and to serve as a resource 25. ability to handle the stress and pressures of training 26. ability to conduct training activities in one's areas of strength; using skilled trainers for other activities where one has more limited skills
International Issues	27. ability to present theories of development, social change, transfer of technology 28. ability to engage learners in thinking about the central issues of international relations, especially as these will affect them personally: dependence versus interdependence, impact of the colonial legacy, parity versus dominance or superiority

Multicultural Issues	29. capacity to provide instruction about cultural pluralism and diversity and on intercultural interactions in the workplace and in society 30. capacity to provide consciousness-raising education about the nature and impact of racism, sexism, and other forms of prejudice and discrimination 31. capacity to design training programs which are sensitive to the history of oppression, discrimination, and intergroup relations of the groups being trained 32. capacity to conceptualize and provide supportive social and psychological mechanisms for dealing with cultural marginality and multiculturalism

Trainer Competencies: Personal Attributes

1. Tolerance of ambiguity
2. Cognitive and behavioral flexibility
3. Personal self-awareness, strong personal identity
4. Cultural self-awareness
5. Patience
6. Enthusiasm and commitment
7. Interpersonal sensitivity
8. Tolerance of differences
9. Openness to new experiences and to people who are different
10. Empathy
11. Sense of humility
12. Sense of humor

COMPETENCIES IN THE
TRAINING AND DEVELOPMENT MODEL

American Society for Training and Development, Washington, D.C.

1. Adult Learning Understanding: Knowing how adults acquire and use knowledge, skills, attitudes. Understanding individual differences in learning.

2. Audio-Visual Skill: Selecting and using audio-visual hardware and software.

3. Career Development Knowledge: Understanding the personal and organizational issues and practices relevant to individual careers.

4. Competency Identification Skill: Identifying the knowledge and skill requirements of jobs, tasks, roles.

5. Computer Competence: Understanding and being able to use computers.

6. Cost-Benefit Analysis Skill: Assessing alternatives in terms of their financial, psychological and strategic advantages and disadvantages.

7. Counseling Skill: Helping individuals recognize and understand personal needs, values, problems, alternative goals.

8. Data Reduction Skill: Scanning, synthesizing and drawing conclusion from data.

9. Delegation Skill: Assigning task responsibility and authority to others.

10. Facilities Skill: Planning and coordinating logistics in an efficient and cost-effective manner.

11. Feedback Skill: Communicating opinions, observations and conclusions so that they are understood.

12. Futuring Skill: Projecting trends and visualizing possible and probable futures and their implications.

13. Group Process Skill: Influencing groups to both accomplish tasks and fulfill the needs of their members.

14. Industry Understanding: Knowing the key concepts and variables that define an industry or sector (e.g., critical issues, economic vulnerabilities, measurements, distribution channels, inputs, outputs, information sources).

15. Intellectual Versatility: Recognizing, exploring and using a broad range of ideas and practices. Thinking logically and creatively without undue influence from personal biases.

16. Library Skills: Gathering information from printed and other recorded sources. Identifying and using information specialists and reference services and aids.

17. Model Building Skill: Developing theoretical and practical frameworks which describe complex ideas in understandable, usable ways.

18. Negotiation Skill: Securing win-win agreements while successfully representing a special interest in a decision situation.

19. Objectives Preparation Skill: Preparing clear statements which describe desired outputs.

20. Organization Behavior Understanding: Seeing organizations as dynamic, political, economic and social systems which have multiple goals; using this larger perspective as a framework for understanding and influencing events and change.

21. Organization Understanding: Knowing the strategy, structure, power networks, financial position, systems of a SPECIFIC organization.

22. Performance Observation Skills: Tracking and describing behaviors and their effects.

23. Personnel and Human Resource Understanding: Understanding issues and practices in other HR areas (Organization Development, Organization Job Design, Human Resource Planning, Selection and Staffing, Personnel Research and Information Systems, Compensation and Benefits, Employee Assistance, Union/Labor Relations).

24. Presentation Skills: Verbally presenting information so that the intended purpose is achieved.

25. Questioning Skill: Gathering information from and stimulating insight in individuals and groups, through the use of interviews, questionnaires and other probing methods.

26. Records Management Skill: Storing data in easily retrievable form.

27. Relationship Versatility: Adjusting behavior in order to establish relationships across a broad range of people and groups.

28. Research Skills: Selecting, developing and using methodologies, statistical and data collection techniques for a formal inquiry.

29. Training and Development Field Understanding: Knowing the technology, social, economic, professional and regulatory issues in the field, understanding the role T&D play in helping individuals learn for current and future jobs.

30. Training and Development Techniques Understanding: Knowing the techniques and methods used in training; understanding their appropriate uses.

31. Writing Skills: Preparing written material which follows generally accepted rules of style and form, is appropriate for the audience, creative and accomplishes its intended purposes.

THE FIFTEEN KEY TRAINING AND DEVELOPMENT ROLES

American Society for Training and Development, Washington, D.C.

This study proposes that the Training and Development (T&D) field consists of people who perform a different mix of roles. Some also perform roles which are outside the T&D areas defined it in this study. The fifteen roles below are those which emerged from literature reviews and after several rounds of review and questionnaires to experts in the T&D field. Some of the roles may be important in other Human Resource (HR) areas. We assume that the competencies required to perform a T&D role will transfer to other areas where that role is important. The extent of transferability is the extent an individual can easily move between and among the human resource area and into jobs outside human resources which require facility in the roles.

The roles below describe the major T&D functions which emerged in this study. They do not describe jobs. Individual jobs usually consist of several or many roles:

- EVALUATOR: The role of identifying the extent of a program, service or product's impact.
- GROUP FACILITATOR: The role of managing group discussions and group process so that individuals learn and group members *feel* the experience is positive.
- INDIVIDUAL DEVELOPMENT COUNSELOR: The role of helping an individual assess personal competencies, values, goals and identify and plan development and career actions.
- INSTRUCTIONAL WRITER: The role of preparing written learning and instructional materials.
- INSTRUCTOR: The role of presenting information and directing structured learning experiences so that individuals learn.
- MANAGER OF TRAINING AND DEVELOPMENT: The role of planning, organizing, staffing, controlling Training and Development operations or Training and Development projects and of linking T&D operations with other organization units.
- MARKETER: The role of selling Training and Development viewpoints, learning packages, programs and services to target audiences outside one's own work unit.
- MEDIA SPECIALIST: The role of producing software for and using audio, visual, computer and other hardware-based technologies for training and development.
- NEEDS ANALYST: The role of defining gaps between ideal and actual performance and specifying the cause of the gaps.
- PROGRAM ADMINISTRATOR: The role of ensuring that the facilities, equipment, materials, participants and other components of a learning event are present and that program logistics run smoothly.
- PROGRAM DESIGNER: The role of preparing objectives, defining content, selecting and sequencing activities for a specific program.
- STRATEGIST: The role of developing long-range plans so that the training and development structure, organization, direction, policies, programs, services, and practices will be in order to accomplish the training and development mission.
- TASK ANALYST: Identifying activities, tasks, sub-tasks, human resource and support requirements necessary to accomplish specific results in a job or organization.

- THEORETICIAN: The role of developing and testing theories of learning, training and development.
- TRANSFER AGENT: The role of helping individuals apply learning after the learning experience.

MEASURING THE TRAINER'S EFFECTIVENESS

L. Robert Kohls

Warmth/friendliness	1	2	3	4	5
Presence/appearance	1	2	3	4	5
Ability to explain clearly	1	2	3	4	5
Seems to enjoy training	1	2	3	4	5
Voice quality/expressiveness	1	2	3	4	5
Mannerisms	1	2	3	4	5
Knowledge of training techniques	1	2	3	4	5
Ability to think on feet	1	2	3	4	5
Sensitivity to effectiveness	1	2	3	4	5
Ability to improvise and change plan when it is not working	1	2	3	4	5
Versatility (can train in many areas)	1	2	3	4	5

Average of all scores _____

Improvement plan: (Any area with a score of three or less should be examined and an action plan developed to improve in that area.)

SELF-DIAGNOSTIC RATING SCALE

COMPETENCIES FOR THE ROLE OF ADULT EDUCATOR/TRAINER

©1975 Malcolm S. Knowles

Indicate on the five-point scale by each of the competencies listed below: (1) the required level for excellent performance of the role you are in now or are preparing for by placing an **R** (for required level) at the appropriate point; (2) the level of your present development of each competency, by placing a **P** (present level) at the appropriate point. For example, if your role is that of teacher, you probably would place the "Rs" for the competencies for the role of learning facilitator higher than you would for the competencies for the role of administrator. You will emerge with a profile of the gaps between where you are now and where you need to be in order to perform your role well.

This is how it would look:

(0) Absent   (1) Low   (2) Low/Mod   (3) Moderate   (4) Mod/High   (5) High

COMPETENCY	COMPETENCY LEVEL
I. As a learning facilitator	
A. Regarding the conceptual and theoretical framework of adult learning:	Absent/Low/Low-Mod/Moderate/Mod-High/High
1. Ability to describe and apply modern concepts and research findings regarding the needs, interests, motivations, capacities, and developmental characteristics of adults as learners.	0 1 2 3 4 5
2. Ability to describe the differences in assumptions about youths and adults as learners and the implications of these differences for teaching.	0 1 2 3 4 5
3. Ability to assess the effects of forces impinging on learners from the larger environment (groups, organizations, cultures) and to manipulate them constructively.	0 1 2 3 4 5
4. Ability to describe the various theories of learning and assess their relevance to particular adult learning situations.	0 1 2 3 4 5
5. Ability to conceptualize and explain the role of teacher as a facilitator and resource person for self-directed learners.	0 1 2 3 4 5

Source: Malcolm S. Knowles. (1975). *Self-directed learning: a guide for learners and teachers.* Chicago, IL: Association Press/Follet.

6. Ability to apply the principles of learning to learn to intercultural communications and the implications of anticipated outcomes.	0 1 2 3 4 5
7. Ability to apply adult learning principles to training and orientation of personnel for service in cross-cultural contexts.	0 1 2 3 4 5
B. Regarding the design and implementing of learning experiences:	Absent/Low/Low-Mod/Moderate/Mod-High/High
1. Ability to describe the difference between a content plan and a process plan.	0 1 2 3 4 5
2. Ability to design learning experiences for accomplishing a variety of purposes that take into account individual differences among learners.	0 1 2 3 4 5
3. Ability to engineer a physical and psychological climate of mutual respect, trust, openness, supportiveness, and safety.	0 1 2 3 4 5
4. Ability to establish a warm, empathic, facilitative relationship with learners of all sorts.	0 1 2 3 4 5
5. Ability to engage learners responsibly in self- diagnosis of needs for learning.	0 1 2 3 4 5
6. Ability to engage learners in formulating objectives that are meaningful to them.	0 1 2 3 4 5
7. Ability to involve learners in the planning, conducting, and evaluating of learning activities appropriately.	0 1 2 3 4 5
C. Regarding helping learners become self-directing:	Absent/Low/Low-Mod/Moderate/Mod-High/High
1. Ability to explain the conceptual difference between didactic instruction and self-directed learning.	0 1 2 3 4 5
2. Ability to design and conduct one-hour, three-hour, one-day, and three-day learning experiences to develop the skills of self-directed learning.	0 1 2 3 4 5
3. Ability to model the role of self-directed learning in your behavior.	0 1 2 3 4 5
4. Ability to facilitate self-directed learner skill development for those anticipating cross-cultural service.	0 1 2 3 4 5

5. Ability to assess application of self-directed learning in the context of cross-cultural work.	0 1 2 3 4 5
6. Ability to interpret the contribution of self-directed learning to the learning context of another culture.	0 1 2 3 4 5
D. Regarding the selection of methods, techniques, and materials:	Absent/Low/Low-Mod/Moderate/Mod-High/High
1. Ability to describe the range of methods or formats for organizing learning experiences.	0 1 2 3 4 5
2. Ability to describe the range of techniques available for facilitating learning.	0 1 2 3 4 5
3. Ability to identify the range of materials available as resources for learning.	0 1 2 3 4 5
4. Ability to provide a rationale for selecting a particular method, technique, or material for achieving particular educational outcomes.	0 1 2 3 4 5
5. Ability to evaluate various methods, techniques, and materials as to their effectiveness in achieving particular educational outcomes.	0 1 2 3 4 5
6. Ability to develop and manage procedures for the construction of models of competency.	0 1 2 3 4 5
7. Ability to construct and use tools and procedures for assessing competency-development needs.	0 1 2 3 4 5
8. Ability to use a wide variety of presentation methods effectively.	0 1 2 3 4 5
9. Ability to use a wide variety of experiential and simulation methods effectively.	0 1 2 3 4 5
10. Ability to use audience-participation methods effectively.	0 1 2 3 4 5
11. Ability to use group dynamics and small group techniques effectively.	0 1 2 3 4 5
12. Ability to invent new techniques to fit new situations.	0 1 2 3 4 5
13. Ability to evaluate learning outcomes and processes and to select or construct appropriate instruments and procedures for this purpose.	0 1 2 3 4 5

14. Ability to confront new situations with confidence and a high tolerance for ambiguity.	0 1 2 3 4 5
15. Ability to apply to intercultural work the selection of appropriate methods, techniques, and materials.	0 1 2 3 4 5

II. As a Program Developer

A. Regarding the planning process:	Absent/Low/Low-Mod/Moderate/Mod-High/High
1. Ability to describe and implement the basic steps (e.g., climate setting, needs assessment, formulation of program objectives, program design, program execution, and evaluation) that undergird the planning process in adult education.	0 1 2 3 4 5
2. Ability to involve representatives of the client systems appropriately in the planning process.	0 1 2 3 4 5
3. Ability to develop and use instruments and procedures for assessing the needs of individuals, organizations, and sub-populations in social systems.	0 1 2 3 4 5
4. Ability to use systems analysis strategies in program planning.	0 1 2 3 4 5
5. Ability to apply the above four points to intercultural work.	0 1 2 3 4 5
B. Regarding the designing and operating of programs:	Absent/Low/Low-Mod/Moderate/Mod-High/High
1. Ability to contrast a wide variety of program designs to meet the needs of various situations (basic skills training, developmental education, supervisory and management development, organizational development, etc.).	0 1 2 3 4 5
2. Ability to design programs with a creative variety of formats, activities, schedules, resources, and evaluative procedures.	0 1 2 3 4 5
3. Ability to use needs assessments, census data, organizational records, surveys, etc., in adapting programs to specific needs and clientele.	0 1 2 3 4 5
4. Ability to use planning mechanisms, such as advisory councils, committees, task forces, etc., effectively.	0 1 2 3 4 5

5. Ability to develop and carry out a plan for program evaluation that will satisfy the requirements of institutional accountability and provide for program improvement.	0 1 2 3 4 5

II. As an Administrator

A. **Regarding organizational development and maintenance:**	Absent/Low/Low-Mod/Moderate/Mod-High/High
1. Ability to describe and apply theories and research findings about organizational behavior, management, and renewal.	0 1 2 3 4 5
2. Ability to develop and carry out a plan for program evaluation that will satisfy the requirements of institutional accountability and provide for program improvement.	0 1 2 3 4 5
3. Ability to formulate policies that clearly convey the definition of mission, social philosophy, educational commitment, etc., of an organization.	0 1 2 3 4 5
4. Ability to evaluate organizational effectiveness and to guide its continuous self-renewal processes.	0 1 2 3 4 5
5. Ability to plan effectively with and through others, sharing responsibilities and decision-making with them as appropriate.	0 1 2 3 4 5
6. Ability to select, supervise, and provide for in-service education of personnel.	0 1 2 3 4 5
7. Ability to evaluate staff performance.	0 1 2 3 4 5
8. Ability to analyze and interpret legislation affecting adult education.	0 1 2 3 4 5
9. Ability to describe financial policies and practices in the field of adult education and to use them as guidelines for setting your own policies and practices.	0 1 2 3 4 5
10. Ability to perform the role of change agent vis a vis organizations and communities utilizing educational processes.	0 1 2 3 4 5
11. Ability to apply the above "abilities" in intercultural work.	0 1 2 3 4 5

B. Regarding Program Administration:	Absent/Low/Low-Mod/Moderate/Mod-High/High
1. Ability to design and operate programs within the framework of a limited budget.	0 1 2 3 4 5
2. Ability to make an monitor financial plans and procedures.	0 1 2 3 4 5
3. Ability to interpret modern approaches to adult education and training to policy-makers convincingly.	0 1 2 3 4 5
4. Ability to design and use promotion, publicity, and public relations strategies appropriately and effectively.	0 1 2 3 4 5
5. Ability to prepare grant proposals and identify potential funding sources for them.	0 1 2 3 4 5
6. Ability to make use of consultants appropriately.	0 1 2 3 4 5
7. Ability and willingness to experiment with programmatic innovations and to assess their results objectively.	0 1 2 3 4 5
8. Ability to innovatively apply to intercultural communications the above competencies.	0 1 2 3 4 5

TRAINING
METHODOLOGIES

SECTION TITLES

INSTRUCTIONAL METHODOLOGIES AND LEARNING STRATEGIES

ADVANTAGES AND DISADVANTAGES OF A DOZEN TEACHING/TRAINING METHODOLOGIES

TRAINING METHODS

INSTRUCTIONAL TECHNIQUES TO IMPART KNOWLEDGE, TO TEACH A SKILL, TO CHANGE ATTITUDES, AND TO ENCOURAGE CREATIVITY

CROSS-CULTURAL TRAINING TECHNIQUES AND METHODOLOGIES

MATCHING TECHNIQUES TO DESIRED BEHAVIORAL OUTCOMES

INSTRUCTIONAL DEVICES

INSTRUCTIONAL METHODOLOGIES AND LEARNING STRATEGIES

L. Robert Kohls

INSTRUCTIONAL METHODS
Teaching Machines
> Programmed Instruction (PI)
>
> Computer-Assisted Instruction (CAI)
>
> Computer-Managed Instruction (CMI)

Learning Activity Package (LAP)

Information-Collecting Assignments

Reading Assignments

Textbooks

Photocopied Handouts

Vertical File

Models

Role Modeling

Lecture
> Lecturette (Mini-Lecture)
>
> Illustrated Presentation

"Sibling" Teaching

Peer Teaching

Relay Teaching

Team Teaching

Co-Teaching Conversation

Question-and-Answer Sessions

Socratic Method

GROUP TECHNIQUES
Panel Discussion

Panel Forum

Veterans' Panel

Colloquy

Symposium

Symposium Forum

Seminar

Conference

Workshop

Clinic

Small Group Discussion

Interviewing Techniques
Brain Storming
Force-Field Analysis
Decision by Consensus
Agree-Disagree Statements
Buzz Groups
Task Force Assignment
Delphi Technique
Micro-Teaching
Fishbowl Meeting
Group-on-Group Meetings
Charette
Structured Experiences
Laboratory Experiments
Human Relations Training (Learning Laboratory)
D-Groups (Developmental Groups [Leader-less Groups])

SIMULATION TECHNIQUES
Case Study Method
    Multiple-Attack Approach
    Maze Technique
Critical Incidents
Problem Solving/Scenario Technique
In-Basket Exercise
Plays/Skits
Role Playing
    Single Role Plays
    Multiple Role Plays
    Role Rotation
    Spontaneous Role Playing
Sociodrama
Non-Verbal Exercises
Games and Simulations
    Game
    Simulation
    Gaming Simulation
    Community Simulation

PRACTICAL EXPERIENCES
Field Trips
Use of Community Resources

Community Analysis

Live-Ins

Third-Cultural Experience

Direct Manipulation Laboratories

Experiment

On-the-Job Training (OJT)

AUDIO-VISUAL SUPPORT SYSTEMS

Chalkboard (Blackboard)

Flip Chart

    Flannel Board

    Charts

    Graphs

    Diagrams

    Illustrations

    Posters

Opaque Projector

Overhead Projector (Vu-Master)

Audio Tape Recorder

Slides/Filmstrip

Sound Slide Film

Films-Motion Pictures (Movies)

Single Concept Film (Loops)

Television

    Closed Circuit Television

Polaroid Camera (Still; Motion)

Videotape Cameras (VTR)

Immediate Playback Critique

EVALUATIVE ACTIVITIES

Individual Reports

Questionnaires

Open-book Exams

Instrumentation

Testing

    Paper-and-Pencil Tests

    Performance Tests

    Simulation Modes

    Interactive Methods

    Norm-Referenced Tests

    Criterion-Referenced Tests

Content-Referenced Tests
Oral Questioning
Critique
Videotape Playback Critique
Multiple Group Presentation
Feedback Session

For descriptions and tips refer to L. Robert Kohls. (1979). *Methodologies for trainers a compendium of learning strategies.* Washington, DC: Future Life Press.

ADVANTAGES AND DISADVANTAGES OF A DOZEN TEACHING/TRAINING METHODOLOGIES

L. Robert Kohls

LECTURE

Plus

- Lots of information
- Likely to be accurate information
- Structured
- Definite beginning and ending
- Definitive
- Comfortable setting for learning
- Can be organized for summary
- Some content fits better into lecture format
- Cheap
- Can address a large group
- Expert lecturer can create interest in topic
- Speedier and economical way to share new information at times
- Can present large amount of content

Minus

- One-way communication
- Can present overlap of information
- Dependent on lecturer (if good or bad)
- Takes longer to integrate information
- Short attention span
- More difficult to retain verbal (cf. visual/experiential)
- Information easily missed
- Impersonal
- Non-participatory
- One-sided information
- Reaches only a certain type of learner
- A great deal of preparation required for a good lecture
- Can put you to sleep (hence less learning)

BRIEFING/DEBRIEFING

Plus

- Time and cost effective
- Direct
- Resolution usually occurs
- Controlled
- Efficient
- Requires little equipment
- Preparation time is minimal
- Brief presentations hold attention of audience (briefing)
- Good processing (to debrief)
- Good introduction
- Great deal of information can be given in a short time
- Develops excellent communication flow within organization
- Goal directed
- Ties multiple ideas together
- Easy to do if you know your subject

Minus

- One-way communication
- Can be too controlled
- Limited to short-term coverage
- No alternate solutions/discussion
- Can easily forget to give
- One time deal
- Superficial
- May not be cost effective
- Easy to manipulate audience
- Often used to sell instead of inform
- Minimal interaction
- For passing information only (not instructions)

INTERVIEW

Plus	Minus
• Very specific information	• Missed information
• Controlled	• Closed questions
• Allows for exchange of information	• Might lead interviewee
• Personal (one on one)	• Lacks spontaneity
• Allows you to observe interpersonal skills	• Bias can show
• Immediate feedback	• Validity of information
• Can change structure according to responses	• Intimidating
• With preparation/research, interview, can bring out more information faster	• Dependent on interviewer's skills
• Reveals more about interviewee	• Misinterpretation very likely
• Better than lecture in that it provides two viewpoints	• Too much depends on first impression
	• Requires good questions (pre-planning)
	• Corny; contrived
	• Observers could feel left out if interview not handled well
	• Interviewer can be manipulative

DISCUSSION

Plus	Minus
• Involves most group members	• Easy to get off track
• Generate many ideas	• Dominance of self-appointed leader or a few members
• Interaction high	• More difficult to control output
• Uses other's experiences	• Time consuming
• More candid expressions	• Some members may be intimidated and not participate
• Synergism	• Risky (input may not be complete)
• Leadership changes	• Requires trainer to stay on track and encourage mass participation
• Attention-grabbing	• Can be boring
• Permits variety of options to be explored	• Effectiveness depends on group's composition
• Varied backgrounds can introduce more possibilities	

CASE STUDY

Plus	Minus
• Real-life application	• May be too general
• Active participation	• May be too abstract
• Holds learner's attention	• Topics may be limited
• Can be effective to teach both technical skills and attitudes	• If poorly written, can be confusing
• Proactive	• Requires skillful trainer
• Serves as good example	• Limited application
• "Real life" example makes it more meaningful	• Can be boring if too lengthy
• Interesting to see other aspects (as others point them out)	• Over-intellectual
• Known outcome (unless case is purposely open-ended)	• Backgrounds of trainees may not be applicable
• Immediate feedback	• Not flexible
• Good test of trainee's skills	

CRITICAL INCIDENT

Plus	Minus
• Skill directed	• Too specific to generalize
• Experiential	• Contrived
• Gives clear focus	• Volatile incident could create hostilities
• Specific	• Could be costly due to limited application to a specific group
• Applicable to real life situation	• Limited application to organization at large
• Resolution of "snags" that could hinder	• Difficult to tie into overall big picture
• Elicits creativity	• Time-consuming
• Serves as good example	• Confusing concept as a methodology
• Individual growth	• Still requires someone to decide whether to implement suggested solution or not, or to select from several possible solutions
• Process oriented	
• Easy to manage training of skill	
• Flexibility	
• Usually effective in bringing out useful change in trainees	

ROLE PLAY

Plus	Minus
• Experiential	• Can be unrealistic
• Holds learner's attention	• Idealistic; limited focus
• Learning by doing (practice of perform-ance)	• Withholding; reluctance to enter into fully
• Forces different role identification	• Intimidating/uncomfortable
• Perceives different opinions	• Lacks resolution
• Spontaneity	• Insensitive use or application could do more damage
• Holds group's attention	• Too risky
• Higher level of retention	• Very difficult
• Discover hidden attitudes	• Dependent on leader for direction/ structure
• Teaches better listening skills and inter-personal skills	• Can be forced to take on unaccept-able role or position
	• Requires preparation for role
	• Must be taken seriously by trainees
	• Depends on trainee's acting ability and imagination
	• Forced participation may limit effec-tiveness

SIMULATION

Plus	Minus
• Practice Session for future skills	• Time required is longer
• Develops attitude and cultural aware-ness	• Less incentive than in actual situation
• Experiential	• The actual simulation can be limiting and unrealistic
• Holds learners' attention	• May be too abstract for some partici-pants to see real world application
• Can be a fun way of learning	• Takes lots of preparation
• Involves everyone's participation	• Difficult to maintain big picture
• More flexible than games	• Meaning (application to real world is lost if trainer doesn't process skill-fully)
• Effective simulation can increase group cohesiveness	
• Open-ended	
• Helps anticipate possible problems	
• Easy to make relevant	
• Can invoke strong feelings	

GAME

Plus	Minus
• Explicit rules	• Explicit rules
• Competition	• Competition
• Good training for dealing with failure	• May get too involved
• Holds learner's attention	• May create unnecessary hostilities
• Fun!	• Must have skilled instructor who can explain application to real life
• An excellent facilitation will help make this a positive learning experience	• Can be unrealistic
• Encourages creativity	• Rules may be constricting
• Encourages interaction	• Time consuming
• High level of retention	• Some participants may feel that the applications are not valuable enough for the time involved
• Encourages informal atmosphere	• Expensive
• Less stressful environment	• Unrealistic expectations of end product
• Holds interest longer	• Discourages interpersonal interaction

FILM/SLIDE SHOW

Plus	Minus
• Can be entertaining	• No interaction
• Provides good backup clarification for a lecture	• One viewpoint
• Adds another sense (sight)	• Equipment laden
• Easier for people to retain information when presented both orally and visually	• Expense
• Easily obtainable	• Time consuming
• Can be multi-sensory: (slide/tape, audio-visual)	• Requires high-level professionalism in production
• Anyone can make film/slide presentations	• Must operate A/V equipment
• Visual stimulation may *reach* more people	• Material becomes quickly outdated
• Provides a wealth of information not easily obtained through lectures	• Limits where to hold session (have to be able to darken room)
• Can be very stimulating	• Not too portable (especially A/V equipment)

VIDEO
(WITH IMMEDIATE PLAYBACK CAPABILITY)

Plus	Minus
• Brings out hidden items	• Gets in the way of presentation
• A permanent record for analysis	• Disruptive to group
• Detailed/fine-tuning	• Equipment can be cumbersome and technical to operate
• See self from trainees' perspective (and as you have never seen yourself before)	• May not work (break)
• Shows how you use space/body language	• Dependent on operator
• Economical for wide distribution	• Can be humiliating or degrading
• Comparison shows growth	• Expensive equipment
• Objective feedback	• Alters behavior of individual being taped
• Can't argue with video	

O J T
(ON-THE-JOB TRAINING)

Plus	Minus
• Individual attention	• Time consuming for supervisor
• Tailored to specific needs	• Lower pay/no benefits
• Learn company methods	• OJT supervisor does not always accept responsibility or share all information
• Immediate application	• Trainee under pressure
• Skill development	• Expensive
• Daily monitoring	• OJT is only as good as the Trainer's and Trainee's self-motivation
• Trainee can ask appropriate questions	• If training time is not adjusted for each trainee there may be unrealistic expectations for training time
• Usually highly motivated	• Traumatic/stressful
• Develop working relationship with colleague	• Can cause resentment from other employees
• Direct displaying of skills	
• Mentorship	
• Networking	
• Looks good on resume	

TRAINING METHODS

Russell D. Robinson

1. Within each general format (individual, group, or community) there are a variety of
    methods or approaches that may be utilized.

FORMAT	METHODS	DESCRIPTION
Individual	Apprenticeship	Under guidance of experienced worker
	Computer-assisted instruction	Interaction with programmed computer
	Correspondence Study	Course by mail with correspondence with instruction
	Counseling	Help from counselor
	Directed Individual Study	Help from instructor from time to time
	Field Experience	Supervised field work
	Independent Reading/Study	Learner-initiated systematic reading and study
	Individual Learning Project	Learner-initiated use of several resources to accomplish specific learning
	Observation/Imitation	Observing and imitating another's performance
	Programmed Learning	Course outlined step by step, with immediate feedback on learning
	Supervision	Help from supervisor
	Tutorial/Coaching	One-on-one with instructor and issues. usually with assistance of discussion leader
Small Group (up to 30)	Class/Course	Series over a period of time
	Clinic	Diagnosis, analysis and solving of problems
	Clubs/Organized Groups	In almost every club one purpose is education of its members
	Colloquium	An advanced group where research projects are planned and evaluates as they progress
	Committee	3 to 7 members with specific task
	Discussion Group	8 to 15 discussing mutual concerns and issues, usually with assistance of discussion leader
	Executive Committee/ Boards	5 to 9 members with general over-seeing responsibilities
	Laboratory Group	8 to 15 studying their own group processes usually with trainer or facilitator
	Residential Learning	Live-in experience of several days
	Round Table	Intensive analysis of a specific

Source: Russell D. Robinson. (1979). *An introduction to helping adults learn and change*. (Revised 1994). West Bend, WI: Omnibook Company. pp. 86-89.

FORMAT	METHODS	DESCRIPTION
Small Group (up to 30)	Seminar	Advanced students in specialized study, learning from discussing their projects and experience with each other.
	Sensitivity Group	8 to 15 helping each other through self-disclosure and feedback, usually with trainer
	Short Course	Abbreviated versions of longer courses, tailored for clientele
	Training Session	Specific skill-building focus
	Task Force	Seeking specific answer or specified result
	Workshop	Emphasis on work sessions, problem-solving, output
Large Group (more than 30)	Assembly	Usually for purpose of agreement on some action
	Conference	One or more days to consider topics using a variety of techniques
	Convention	Usually several days with total group and smaller group sessions bringing together local members in a district, state or national meeting
	Forum	Usually presentation of information followed by audience questions and participation
	Institute	Concentrated sessions, usually over several days, for development of knowledge or skill in a specialized area
	Lecture Series	A lecture course with same or different speakers over period of time
	Meeting	One- to three-hour sessions
	Orientation Sessions	To provide information to a new group
	Work Conference	Working on problems rather than considering topics
Community	Community Action Groups	For purpose of taking action in the community
	Community Development	A process involving the community in its own development and improvement
	Community Problem-solving Groups	For purpose of solving problem
	Community Projects	For purpose of accomplishing a project
	Exhibits, Fairs	For purpose of displaying wares, accomplishments
	Result Demonstration	For purposes of displaying results

INSTRUCTIONAL TECHNIQUES TO IMPART KNOWLEDGE

Russell D. Robinson

1. Techniques appropriate for ONE RESOURCE PERSON PRESENTATIONS to inform, give information, disseminate knowledge, develop understanding:

Technique	Description	Room Arrangement
Committee Hearing	Questioning of a resource person by a panel of interviewers for extemporaneous responses.	
Film	One-way organized presentation.	
Interview	Questioning of a resource person by an individual on behalf of audience.	
Lecture, Speech	One-way organized formal presentation of information or point of view by resource person.	
Lecture with Group Response Team (Audience Reaction Team)	Several group representatives interrupt resource person at appropriate times for immediate clarification of issues.	
Screened Speech	Sub-groups develop questions they wish resource person to address extemporaneously.	

Source: Russell D. Robinson. (1979). *An introduction to helping adults learn and change*. (Revised 1994). West Bend, WI: Omnibook Company.

2. Techniques appropriate for SEVERAL RESOURCE PERSON Presentations to in-
    form, give information, disseminate knowledge, develop understanding:

Technique	Description	Room Arrangement
Colloquy	Panels of 3 or four resource persons and 3 or 4 representatives of the audience discussing issue	
Debate	Conflicting views stated by each resource person and clarified further by argument between them.	
Dialog	Informal, conversational discourse between 2 resource persons.	
Dramatic Presentation	Prepared play or skit to inform.	
Interrogator Panel	2 to 4 resources persons questioned by 2 to 4 interrogators.	
Panel Discussion	Panel of 4 to 7 person carry on a discussion of an issue before an audience (informal discussion "overheard" by audience).	
Symposium	3 to 6 speeches or lectures presented in turn by resource persons on various phases of a single subject or problem.	

3. Techniques appropriate as FOLLOW-UPS to presentations of one or more resource persons to involve the audience:

Technique	Description	Room Arrangement
Buzz Groups	Sub-groups of 4 to 6 with 4 to 6 minutes to discuss particular issue or question raised by resource person.	
Chain Reaction Forum	Sub-groups discuss presentation and formulate questions to be asked resource person.	
Forum	Free and open question/ discussion period immediately following a lecture.	
Group Discussion	Sub-groups of 10 to 20 discuss problems or issues raised, for 15 to 30 minutes.	
Huddle Groups	Pairs or triads (2 to 3 persons/ groups) discuss specific issue for 2 to 3 minutes.	
Listening Team	3 to 4 members in audience are designated to listen and raise questions after presentation.	
Question Period	Opportunity for any in audience to directly question speaker.	
Reaction Panel	Panel of 3 or 4 react to presentation by panel discussion.	
Reaction Symposium	3 or 4 persons in turn give their reaction to presentation.	
Screening Panel	3 or 4 persons screen questions raised by audience (on cards) before presenting questions to resource person.	

Instructional Techniques to Teach a Skill

1.   Techniques appropriate to teach a skill or change a behavior:

Technique	Description
Case Study	Presentation of a problem or case for a small group to analyze and solve
Demonstration	Instructor verbally explains and performs an act, procedure or process
Games, Structured Experiences	Under leadership of instructor, learners participate in a "game" requiring particular skills
Simulation	Learners learn skills in a setting that simulates the real setting where skills are required
Teaching/Learning Team	Working cooperatively, small groups of 3 to 6 persons each teach and help each other develop skills

2.   Techniques appropriate for FOLLOW-UP and practice of skills.

Technique	Description
Application Projects	Performance contracts, check lists, specific exercises to apply learning "back home"
Drill	Practice beyond the point needed for recall to produce automatic response
Practice	Repeated performance of a skill under supervision of instructor, and then without supervision

Instructional Techniques to Change Attitudes

1.   Attitudes are most likely to be changed in a context of free and open discussion, in a climate of trust. In such a climate assumptions and attitudes can be examined with less threat and defensive behavior.

2.   Techniques appropriate to change attitudes, values, opinions, feelings:

Technique	Description
Circle Response	Question posed to members of a group seated in a circle, each person in turn expressing a response.
Exercises, Structured Experiences	Experiencing or viewing actual situations for first hand observation and study.
Field Trips, Tours	Experiencing or viewing actual situations for first hand observation and study.
Games	Experiencing a game and discussing its application to real life.
Group Discussion	Circle face to face mutual exchange of ideas and opinions by members of small groups (8 to 20) on problem or issue of mutual concern for 10 to 40 minutes, depending on size of group.
Process Group (T-Groups, Laboratory Groups	Circle of 8 to 12 people studying themselves in process of becoming and being a group.
Role Playing	Impromptu dramatization of a problem or situation, followed by discussion.
Sensitivity Group	Circle of 8 to 12 people helping each other through self-disclosure and feedback.
Simulation	Experience in a situation as near real as possible, followed by discussion.
Skit	Short rehearsed dramatic presentation, followed by discussion.

3. Virtually every technique listed above requires PROCESS TIME, opportunity for learners to evaluate, discuss, and process the experience.

Instructional Techniques to Encourage Creativity

Technique	Description
Brain storming (ideation: idea inventory)	Free flowing an uninhibited sharing and listing of ideas by a group without evaluation or consideration of practicality; object is to generate as many creative ideas as possible.
Nominal Group Process	A specific procedure for a group of 5 to 8 people for maximum idea generation and narrowing the range of ideas: 1. Each person makes his own list of ideas (5 to 10 minutes). 2. Master list is made on newsprint in round robin fashion as each contributes one idea to list until *all* ideas are on master list (10 to 15 minutes). 3. Clarification (but not discussion) of items on master list (15 minutes). 4. Each person chooses 5 items from the master list without discussion (5 minutes). 5. Each person ranks 5 items and accords value points (5 for first, four for second, 3 for third, 2 for fourth, 1 for fifth. 6. "Votes" (value points) are recorded for each item on master list. 7. Ideas receiving the most points are discussed.
Quiet Meeting (Quaker Meeting)	15 to 60 minute period of reflection and limited verbal expression by group members; periods of silence and spontaneous verbal contributions.
Self-Analysis and Reflection	Time allocated for personal reflection and opportunity to relax and examine learning alone.

TWO-AXIS CHART OF CROSS-CULTURAL TRAINING TECHNIQUES AND METHODOLOGIES

Alexander Patico

DESCRIPTION: Selected techniques are arranged according to two axes:

1. A continuum between two types of goals for training—from *cognitive* (related to *thought*, the abstract, the rational) to *behavioral* (related to action, the concrete, the functional).

2. Defined by the poles *mechanistic* and *organismic*, used to describe different approaches to training—in which the subject is seen either as a "learning machine" or, in the latter, as a "person" in a holistic sense.

PLACEMENT OF THE ITEMS: One should not take the arrangement shown as definitive, but merely illustrative. To give one example: films or video can be employed in a variety of ways with training groups, hence they could appropriately be placed at any point across a broad swath of the chart. At the same time, they are placed where they are because they would not be as exclusively cerebral as, say, the transcripted version—they include a direct impact on the senses and hence affect the viewer on many levels; they would not require as much of the viewer in terms of behavior, as would be the case if the script were acted out by the trainees themselves; and they would usually not lead to very specific, easily testable learnings (unless they were perhaps a video version of language-learning tapes, with a carefully orchestrated progression of items being introduced, placed in context and reviewed). They seem to fit in a particular region of the universe represented by the chart.

POSSIBLE USES: As techniques are being selected for a given setting, the trainer needs to consider the previous learning experience and unique capacities of the particular trainees involved. Typically, there is a range of both represented in any given group. Some subjects are more comfortable with "touchy-feely" techniques; others are prone to intellectualize. Some learn best when placed in an "immersion" situation; others are immobilized by such an assault on their shaky sense of self.

If the techniques being considered can be seen as falling at a point on a continuum (or, in this instrument, two different continua) one can consciously select **a particular sector of the chart** to suit a limited training purpose, or a variety in order to "cover" a diverse set of needs, or **a deliberate weighting** in one direction or another in order to tailor the training experience to compensate for deficits, to accommodate weaknesses, to build unused cognitive "muscles", or to create a (controlled) stress-producing environment.

CAUTION: Each technique taken together with its specific content, the overall training context, the skills of the trainers. and other circumstances must be analyzed to determine the real anticipated impact.

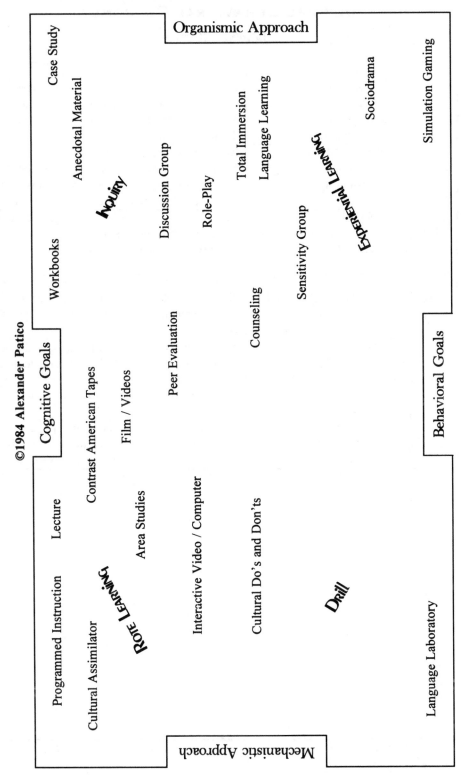

CROSS-CULTURAL TRAINING TECHNIQUES AND METHODOLOGIES

©1984 Alexander Patico

Organismic Approach

Cognitive Goals

Behavioral Goals

Mechanistic Approach

ROTE LEARNING

INQUIRY

EXPERIENTIAL LEARNING

DRILL

Case Study

Anecdotal Material

Total Immersion
Language Learning

Sociodrama

Simulation Gaming

Workbooks

Discussion Group

Role-Play

Sensitivity Group

Lecture

Contrast American Tapes

Film / Videos

Peer Evaluation

Counseling

Programmed Instruction

Cultural Assimilator

Area Studies

Interactive Video / Computer

Cultural Do's and Don'ts

Language Laboratory

MATCHING TECHNIQUES TO DESIRED BEHAVIORAL OUTCOMES

Malcolm S. Knowles

Type of Behavior Outcome	Most Appropriate Techniques
KNOWLEDGE (Generalizations about experience; internalization of information)	Lecture, television, debate, dialogue, interview, symposium, panel group interview, colloquy, motion picture, slides, recording, book-based discussion, reading.
UNDERSTANDING (Application of information and generalizations)	Audience participation, demonstration, motion picture, dramatization, Socratic discussion, problem-solving discussion, case discussion, critical incident process, case method, games.
SKILLS (Incorporation of new ways of performing through practice)	Role playing, in-basket exercises, games, action mazes, participative cases, T-Group, nonverbal exercises, skill practice exercises, drill, coaching.
ATTITUDES (Addition of new feelings through experiencing greater success with them rather than with old)	Experience-sharing discussion, group-centered discussion, role playing, critical incident process, case method, game, participative cases, T-Group, nonverbal exercises.
VALUES (The adoption and priority arrangement of beliefs)	Television, lecture (sermon), debate, dialogue, symposium, colloquy, motion picture, dramatization, guided discussion, experience-sharing discussion, role playing, critical incident process, games, T-Groups.
INTERESTS (Satisfying exposure to new activities)	Television, demonstration, motion picture, slides, dramatization, experience-sharing discussion, exhibits, trips, nonverbal exercises.

Source: Malcolm S. Knowles. (1970). *The modern practice of adult education.* Associated Press, p. 294.

INSTRUCTIONAL DEVICES

Russell D. Robinson

1. There are many instructional devices (also called instructional aids or instructional materials) available today.

2. Below are grouped such devices from the most concrete and experiential, in directly involving the learner, to the more abstract, relying on verbal symbols (words) alone.

3. Note that audio-visual aids are *not* more effective than experiential devices.

Instructional Devices

CONCRETE

Worksheets, observation guides, manuals, workbooks
Models, mock-ups, objects, specimens
In-basket exercises, structured experiences, games, critical incidents, case studies

Experiential

Skits, plays, puppetry, simulations
Video tapes, television
Films, slide films with sound

Audio-visual

Audio-tapes, records, radio, recording and playback devices
Slides, film strips, projected still pictures
Overhead projection, opaque projection of charts, diagrams, graphs, photographs, etc.
Photographs, maps, posters, drawings, charts, etc.
Chalkboards, cork boards, flipcharts, flannel boards, hook and loop

Visual or audio

Information briefs, summaries, handouts, study guides, programmed texts
Publications, books, pamphlets, newspapers, magazine articles, annotated reading lists

Written

ABSTRACT

Source: Russell D. Robinson. (1979). *An introduction to helping adults learn and change.* (Revised 1994). West Bend, WI: Omnibook Company.

STAND-UP

TRAINING SKILLS

or

PLATFORM SKILLS

SECTION TITLE

TRAINER PLATFORM SKILLS

TRAINER PLATFORM SKILLS

Coleman Finkel

The approach, technique and skills needed to give an effective talk at a conference are significantly different than those necessary to deliver a presentation at a training session. There are different skills needed to speak effectively to a large group as compared to instructing at a small training meeting.

Large Group Skills

The following considerations make a speaker effective before a large group:

1. A commanding theatrical style is desirable to hold the audience's attention. Gestures must be exaggerated.
2. When visuals are used, the visuals need to be either dramatic or large enough to be seen by attendees spread throughout a room.
3. The ability to modulate, control and project one's voice is a necessity before a large audience.
4. The speaker must recognize that many audience-participation techniques, which are valid in small groups, are lost in large groups and, therefore, require a modification if they are to be used at all. It is more difficult for an attendee in a large group to feel a part of the total group.
5. One needs to develop speaking skill. Word-for-word reading from a paper will put an audience to sleep.
6. Material must be organized around a few key ideas. The audience will be unable to concentrate if the speaker tries too incorporate to much information in the talk.

Small Group Skills

On the other hand, these are the styles, skills and materials needed by successful trainers before small audiences of 15 to 25 people:

1. The ability to probe, provoke, parry with the members of a group so that each person is challenged to think.
2. Developing participation techniques to engage the group individually or in teams to apply the information to their own jobs and companies.
3. Writing effectively on chalkboards, chart pads or on overhead film projectors so the group can follow program highlights and use them as a springboard for more pointed questions and contributions.
4. Staying alert to audience participation and skillfully drawing into the discussion all members of the group.
5. Summarizing discussions frequently so audience is continually provided with points of reference so further discussion can proceed with continuity and common understanding.
6. Organizing presentations with focus, practicality, and stimulation.
7. Handling questions at any time without losing continuity of a presentation.

Adapted from: Coleman Finkel. (1978). "Speaker vs. trainer platform skills," in *Training and Development Journal,* ASTD, November 1978.

SEATING

ARRANGEMENT

or

ROOM

ARRANGEMENT

SECTION TITLE

ROOM ARRANGEMENTS

ROOM ARRANGEMENTS

Russell D. Robinson

1. Theater Style	2. Herringbone Style
3. U-shape Style	**4. Diamond Style**
5. Hexagon Style	**6. Conference Style**
7. Chairs in Circle	**8. Classroom Style**
9. Chairs in Small Semicircles	**10. Banquet Style**

DESIGNING
the
INDIVIDUAL
TRAINING
SESSION

SECTION TITLES

ORGANIC MODEL FOR A LEARNING DESIGN
TRAINING "PACKAGE" (INCLUDING A SAMPLE TRAINING PACKAGE)

ORGANIC MODEL FOR A LEARNING DESIGN

Malcolm S. Knowles

1. Climate setting
2. Establishing a structure for mutual planning
3. Diagnosing needs and interests
4. Formulating objectives
5. Designing a pattern of activities
6. Carrying out the activities
7. Evaluating the results and re-diagnosing needs and interests

Source: Malcolm S. Knowles. (1970). *The modern practice of adult education.* New York: Association Press, p. 190, 291.

TRAINING PACKAGE

L. Robert Kohls

1. Unit Title
2. Order Number (Sequence)
3. Trainer(s)
4. Aims/objectives
5. Estimated total time (hours and/or minutes)
6. Format
   Including:
   > SPECIFIC LEARNING ACTIVITIES AND TECHNIQUES/MEDIA
   > APPROACH/DESCRIPTION
   > SEQUENCE
   > TIME for each activity
   > CONTENT
   > INSTRUMENTS
   > TRAINERS (if more than one)
   > RESOURCE PEOPLE
   > PROCESS QUESTIONS
7. Handouts
8. Designer(s)

—S-A-M-P-L-E—
TRAINING PACKAGE

UNIT DESCRIPTION for: RACISM/SEXISM/CLASSISM
Order Number

TRAINERS:
Lead-Trainer: Kohls and all process-group leaders

AIMS
1. To call attention to (and to increase awareness of) sexism, racism, and classism as it affects all of us in America.

2. To encourage face-to-face discussion (between males and females, blacks and whites) of the problems which separate us.

3. To learn that racial, sexist and class struggles have in common a struggle to wrest or retain power.

4. To afford practice in resolving real differences between existing power-factions.

ESTIMATED TIME (overall) Full day

FORMAT
9:00 AM: View two Films

Salt of the Earth (1 hour)

Wilmington (15 minutes)

No discussion at this time (refer to later in Small Group processing meetings)

10:30 AM: Go directly into SEXISM-NEGOTIATION EXERCISE

Separate volunteers into two groups: Male and Female

Each group meets independently

Ask such questions as:

1. *How does it feel to be in this group of all women (men)?*

2. *What do you think the other group is like?*

3. *How do we want the other group to behave differently toward us?*

This must be translated into a LIST OF DEMANDS.

12 Noon:

Each group to send three representatives to FISHBOWL, the presentation of each side's demands of the other side:

Each side to give the other side:

1. Our perception of you

2. Our demands

Simple presentation (no elaboration at this time).

12:30 PM: Lunch: a working lunch period

Assignment: to ask:

1. *How are we going to respond to their demands?*

2. *How are we willing to modify our own demands?*

2:30 PM:

Second FISHBOWL (1 hour)

- Same 3 representatives from each side (have full power to negotiate)
- Plus 1 empty chair (for outside representatives to come in and contribute as chair empties)
- Each group can send in notes to its representatives
- Assignment: to resolve the issues (This is, of course, impossible in such a short time, but it provides abundant material to discuss in the Small Group processing meetings which follow.)

    1. *How we are responding to your demands?*

    2. *How we are modifying our demands?*

3:30 to 5:30 PM: Back into Small Groups to process

- *How did you feel when the 3 representatives were making decisions for you?*
- Ask the three representatives: *How did you feel making those decisions for the others?*

    Make point that BLACK/WHITE, MALE/FEMALE, and RICH/POOR conflicts are all Power Struggles. If they weren't, the *have* groups wouldn't be so determined to keep the *system* set up the way it is.

As time allows

- Discuss the films that were shown in the morning.

Process reactions to the whole day's activities

HANDOUTS

Gold Flower's Story and *Sex and Revolution* from Jack Belden: China Shakes the World.

The Flint Sitdown Strike

DESIGNER(S)

Lead-Trainer with entire UYA training staff

WORKING
WITH
SMALL
GROUPS

SECTION TITLES

THE ROLE OF THE GROUP FACILITATOR
(WITH EMPHASIS ON HANDLING SPECIFIC PROBLEMS)
RECURRING GROUP ROLES
DYSFUNCTIONAL BEHAVIORS IN GROUPS
(AND FACILITATOR INTERVENTIONS TO DEAL WITH THEM)

THE ROLE OF THE GROUP FACILITATOR

(with Emphasis on Handling Specific Problems)
L. Robert Kohls and Warren Obluck

The group leader—in most cases, you—has a role to play. It might be called Group Facilitator. Both formally and informally the facilitator encourages and makes possible maximum participation by individual group members.

Unless you are unusually domineering (a far from desirable trait in group dynamics) one or two of the participants can be expected, probably unconsciously, to try to wrest informal leadership from you, making the strength of their personalities rather than their contributions pivotal to the discussion. At first glance this may seem unobjectionable. But the fact is that your position as leader must be established unequivocally if you are to be in a position to carry out your responsibilities to the group as a whole.

Therefore, when you detect evidence of this phenomenon, do not let them pass unchallenged. If an *Information Processor* seems to be summarizing a presentation, break in (politely and appropriately) to suggest that a summary seems to be in order and encourage the speaker to provide one. If a *Harmonizer* tries to bring together opposing points of view, explain to the group what he or she has done and ask if the group can suggest still other ways of mediating. Unless you establish your leadership role with task-oriented and supportive role players you will be in a weaker position to deal with destructive role players.

None of this is to suggest that you should be defensive or that you must dominate the group with a heavy hand. But as the program's manager, your script requires you to continue to move the program towards its objectives. No other member of the group can be expected or relied on to do so. Knowing what roles are likely to develop within the group (usually within the first day or two) allows you to identify what members are in which roles and to prepare to deal with them as necessary.

Conducting Discussions: It is important for you to maintain neutrality during presentations. Your first job is not to side with either speaker or audience but to help assure that full discussion takes place.

1. Get the Discussion Started: Start it on time. Your opening remarks should set the style of the conversation by their brevity and directness. Ask a question you think most likely to start discussion. If this fails, ask another.

2. Keep the Discussion on Track: The tendency of discussions to ramble creates a perplexing problem. If you let the discussion wander wherever chance remarks may take it, you are not fulfilling your function. If you hold too rigidly to an outline and appear to dictate the course of conversation, your audience will feel it is being overly controlled. Be cautious in announcing that the discussion is off track, you may have to reverse yourself if members point out relationships that are not apparent to you. The best procedure is to ask whether the discussion is on the subject and to let the group or the speaker decide.

3. Make Occasional Summaries: Use summaries during the discussions to (1) check needless repetition, (2) bring random conversation back to the subject, (3) record apparent areas of agreement or disagreement. Make the summaries brief, impartial and in the language of the group. Resist any impulse to magnify disagreement or to assume agreement when none exists. Insure accuracy and lack of bias by asking the

audience to check you and to add points you may have overlooked. Occasionally, you may want to ask a participant to summarize.

4. Encourage General Participation: It is not essential that every one talk, but it is important that anyone with something to say be encouraged to say it. Try to make it easy for people to talk by acting and speaking yourself as though you expect it.

   It may be a mistake to single out a member for a pointed question. If he or she has nothing to say at the moment the person may be embarrassed and even less likely to speak up later. Timid members may be drawn into the discussion by asking them for specific information you know they have. Inquire whether those who haven't spoken would like to comment and, instead of calling on more vocal audience members, recognize those who have kept silent but look ready to speak. Or you might make a statement, and ask how many agree with it, using the visible responses as an excuse to ask reticent members why they agree or disagree.

5. Get to the Root of the Matter: You may find that your audience is chatting pleasantly, voicing casual opinions, but skirting the real issue. When you feel that the discussion is not getting below the surface, attempt through probing questions to call attention to lack of evidence, the evasion of basic issues, or weakness in reasoning.

6. Remain in the Background: Suggest rather than direct, ask questions instead of answering them. Make your questions pointed and specific. Start with *what* to get opinions and facts, *why* for reasons and causes, *who* or *where* for sources of opinions and facts, and *how* or *when* to narrow the discussion and get down to specific cases. Encourage sharing of leadership throughout the group. If you are the only one asking questions, your role will become too dominant.

Here are some suggestions for questions that can be used to help discussion along. You may find them less useful for their incisiveness than for the tips they contain on problems you may encounter and starting points for dealing with them. In any case, they are meant to be illustrative of the way questions can be used to exercise your leadership and facilitative functions:

a. To call attention to a point that has not been considered: *Has anyone thought about this phase of the problem?*

b. To question the strength of an argument: *What reasons do we have for accepting this position?*

c. To get back to causes: *Why do you suppose Fulano takes this position?*

d. To question the source of information or argument: *Who gathered those statistics that you spoke of? Who is Mr. X, whose opinion you quoted? Do you know that as a fact or is it your opinion?*

e. To suggest that the discussion is wandering from the point: *Can someone tell me how this relates specifically to our problem? Your point is a good one, but can you relate it more closely to the subject?*

f. To suggest that new information is being added: *Can anyone add anything to the information already given on this point?*

g. To call attention to the difficulty or complexity of the problem: *Aren't we beginning to understand why Management hasn't solved this Problem?*

h. To bring the generalizing speaker down to earth: *Can you give us a specific example on that point? Your general idea is good, but I wonder if we can make it more concrete? Does anyone know a case…?*

i.   To register steps of agreement (or disagreement): *Am I correct in assuming that we all agree (disagree) on this point?*

j.   To handle the impatient, cure-all member: *But would your plan work in all cases? Who has an idea on that? Hadn't we better reserve judgment until we hear our speaker out?*

k.   To suggest that personalities be avoided: *I wonder what bearing that has on the question before us?*

l.   To suggest that some are talking too much: *Aren't there those who haven't spoken who have ideas they would like to present?*

m.   To suggest the need for compromise: *Doesn't the best course of action lie somewhere between these two points of view?*

n.   To suggest that the group may be prejudiced: *Isn't our personal interest in this question causing us to overlook the interests of other groups?*

o.   To draw the timid but informed member into the discussion: *Lovelace, here, worked for quite a while in Southeast Asia. Let's ask him whether he ever...*

p.   To handle a question you (or the speaker) can't answer: *I don't know. Who does?* (If no one does know, offer to try to find the specific information then follow through.)

q.   To encourage the speaker to talk with the audience, not at you: *I think they'll hear you a little better if you face the group.*

r.   To cut off a speaker who is too long-winded: While we're on this point, let's hear from some of the others. Can we save your other points until later?

s.   To take the play away from a verbose audience member: *You've raised a number of interesting points which should keep us busy a good while. Who else would like to comment on them?*

t.   To help the member who has difficulty expressing him or herself: *I wonder if what you're saying isn't this...? Doesn't what you've said tie in with our subject something like this...?*

u.   To encourage further questions by friendly comment: *That's a good question. I'm glad you raised it. Anyone have an answer?*

v.   To break up an argument: *I think we all know how Fulano and Jones feel about this. Now who else would like to raise a point?*

In using questions or other techniques to call attention to weaknesses in evidence, procedure, or participation, be careful to avoid statements that indicate your own opinions unless you are serving also as a resource person.

RECURRING GROUP ROLES

Author Unknown

People who work with several different groups are often initially surprised to discover how similar each group is in its composition. Each seems to have people who try to obstruct, for whatever reasons, and others who instinctively try to facilitate the learning process and the smooth functioning of the group. Some of the key roles which you might identify in group after group are:

Task-Oriented Roles
Initiator
Information Seeker / Information Processor
Coordinator
Orientor / Evaluator

Supportive Roles
Encourager / Harmonizer
Tension Reliever
Expeditor
Standard Setter
Follower

Destructive Roles
Blocker
Recognition Seeker
Dominator / Avoider

DYSFUNCTIONAL BEHAVIORS IN GROUPS AND FACILITATOR INTERVENTIONS TO DEAL WITH THEM

Anthony J. Reilly and John E. Jones

Listed below are the commonly observed behaviors that tend to obstruct team development, including ways of coping with the behaviors in a productive way.

Saboteur

This is a person who engages in behaviors designed to destroy or significantly impair the progress made by the team. Examples: *Got'cha behavior*, *Wait until J B sees what you're up to*, *Yes, but...*, and *This will never work!*

Sniper

A person who takes cheap shots at group members (whether they are present or not) by throwing verbal or nonverbal *barbs* is likely to lessen the productivity of the group. For example, the *sniper* might say, *"When we were talking about plant expansion, old J B (who always ignores such issues) made several points, all of which were roundly refuted."*

Assistant Trainer

This is a team member who wants to demonstrate his awareness of group process by making interventions in order to *make points* with the consultant. He/she may make procedural suggestions to the point of being obnoxious. One of his favorite interventions is, *Don't tell me what you think, tell me how you feel!*

Denier

This person plays the *"Who, me?"* game. When confronted, he backs off immediately. He may also ask many questions to mask his statements or points of view, and he generally refuses to take a strong stand on a problem.

Quiet Member

Quiet members may be quiet for innumerable reasons. It has been remarked about silence: *It is never misquoted, but it is often misinterpreted.*

Anxious Member

He/she may engage in such counter-productive behaviors as smoothing over conflict, avoiding confrontation, doodling, *red-crossing* other members, and protecting the leader.

Dominator

Some team members simply take up too much air time. By talking too much, they control the group through their verbosity.

Side-Tracker

This person siphons off the group's energy by bringing up new concerns (deflecting) rather than staying with the problem being worked. Under his/her influence, groups can rapidly generate an enormous list of superfluous issues and concerns and become oblivi-

---

Source: Anthony J. Reilly and John E. Jones. "Team building." *Annual Handbook for Group Facilitators*, pp. 234-236.

ous to the problem at hand. The game he/she plays is generally something like, *Oh, yeah, and another thing ...*

Hand-Clasper

Legitimacy and safety can be borrowed by agreeing with other people. For example, this person says, *I go along with Tom when he/she says ...*

Polarizer

A person who points out difference among team members rather than helping them see sameness in the ownership of group problems can prevent the development of group cohesion. He/she is a person likely to have a predisposition toward seeing mutually exclusive points of view.

Attention-Seeker

This behavior is designed to cover the group member's anxiety by excessive joking, horsing-around, and drawing attention to himself/herself. He/she may do this very subtly by using the personal pronoun *I* often. He/she may also be a person who describes many of his own experiences in an attempt to look good to other group members.

Clown

This person engages in disruptive behavior of a loud, boisterous type. He/she may set a tone of play rather than of problem-solving.

Confronting Dysfunctional Behaviors

The characters described briefly above have one common theme: Each inhibits and distracts the group from working at an optimal level.

In dealing with such dysfunctional roles, the facilitator will find it helpful to follow three general steps.

1. He/she should draw attention to the dysfunctional behavior itself but avoid the trap of labeling or classifying the person as, for example, a *sniper* or a *hand-clasper*. Such evaluative labeling only elicits defensiveness from the individual. Instead, the behavior that is getting in the group's way should be described.

2. The consultant should spell out what appear to be the specific dysfunctional effects of the behavior. This should not be done in a punitive fashion, but in a supportive, confrontive manner. Often the person distracting the group is unaware of the negative impact of his/her behavior. Sometimes he/she really wants to be making a contribution and does not know how to be an effective team member.

3. Alternative behaviors should be suggested which will lead to a more productive and satisfying climate for the disruptive person and his/her colleagues.

FACILITATOR INTERVENTIONS

Process Interventions

Centering around the on-going work of the group as it engages in problem-solving activities, process interventions include ones aimed at improving the team's task accomplishment as well as helping to build the group into a more cohesive unit.

Process interventions to heighten task accomplishment include the following examples:

- having the group translate an issue into a problem statement

- observing that the group is attending to several problems simultaneously rather than sticking to one problem at a time
- observing that a decision was made out of a *hearing-no-objections* norm and having the group deal with this posture
- inviting the group to develop action plans related to a problem solution
- suggesting that the group summarize what has been covered within a given problem-solving period
- helping the group to monitor its own style, using its resources
- using instruments, questionnaires, and ratings to assess the group's position on a particular topic

Process interventions aimed at group maintenance or group building include the following examples:

- pointing out dysfunctional behaviors which keep the group from achieving a cohesive climate
- encouraging group members to express feelings about decisions the group makes
- encouraging group members to respond to one another's ideas and opinions verbally, whether in terms of agreement or disagreement
- confronting behaviors that lead to defensiveness and lack of trust among group member, e.g., evaluative feedback and hidden agendas
- verbally reinforcing group-building behaviors such as gate-keeping, harmonizing, etc.

Structural Interventions

Another class of intervention is termed structural because it deals with the way group members are arranged physically as a group. Structural interventions include the following:

- having group members work privately—making notes to themselves, for example-before they discuss the topic jointly as a total group
- having members pair off to interview each other about the problem
- forming subgroups to explore the different aspects of the problem and then share their work with the remainder of the group
- forming a group-on-group design, to enable an inner group to work independently of an outer group, which, in turn, gives process feedback to inner-group members

FEEDBACK

SECTION TITLES

AIDS FOR GIVING AND RECEIVING FEEDBACK
THE EIGHT RULES OF FEEDBACK

AIDS FOR GIVING AND RECEIVING FEEDBACK

Author Unknown

Some of the most important data we can receive from others (or give to others) consists of feedback related to our behavior. Such feedback can provide learning opportunities for each of us if we can use the reactions of others as a mirror for observing the consequences of our behavior. Such personal data feedback helps to make us more aware of what we do and how we do it, thus increasing our ability to modify and change our behavior and to become more effective in our interactions with others.

To help us develop and use the techniques of feedback for personal growth it is necessary to understand certain characteristics of the process. The following is a brief outline of some factors which may assist us in making better use of feedback, both as the giver and receiver of feedback. This list is only a starting point. You may wish to add further items to it.

1. Focus feedback on behavior rather than on the person.

It is important that we refer to what a person does rather than comment on what we imagine he/she is. This focus on behavior further implies that we use adverbs (which relate to actions) rather than adjectives (which relate to qualities) when referring to a person. Thus we might say a person *talked considerably in this meeting*, rather than that this person *is a loudmouth*. When we talk in terms of *personality traits* it implies inherited constant qualities difficult, if not impossible, to change. Focusing on behavior implies it is something related to a specific situation that might be changed. It is less threatening to a person to hear comments about his/her behavior than his/her *traits*.

2. Focus feedback on observation rather than inferences.

Observations refer to what we can see or hear in the behavior of another person, while inferences refer to interpretations and conclusions which we make from what we see or hear. In a sense, inferences or conclusions about a person contaminate our observations, thus clouding the feedback for another person. When inferences or conclusions are shared, and it may be important to have this data, it is important that they be so identified.

3. Focus feedback on description rather than on judgment.

The effort to describe represents a process for reporting what occurred, while judgment refers to an evaluation in terms of *good* or *bad*, *right* or *wrong*, *nice* or *not nice*. The judgments arise out of a personal frame of reference or values, whereas description represents neutral (as far as possible) reporting.

4. Focus feedback on descriptions of behavior which are in terms of *more or less* rather than in terms of *either/or*.

The *more or less* terminology implies a continuum on which any behavior may fall, stressing quantity, which is objective and measurable, rather than quality, which is subjective and judgmental. Thus, participation of a person may fall on a continuum from low participation to high participation, rather than *good* or *bad* participation. Not to think in terms of *more* or *less* and the use of continua is to trap ourselves into thinking in categories, which then may represent serious distortions of reality.

5. Focus feedback on behavior related to a specific situation, preferably to the *here and now*, rather than to behavior in the abstract, placing it in the *there and then*.

What you and I do is always tied in some way to time and place, and we increase our understanding of behavior by keeping it tied to time and place. Feedback is generally more meaningful if given as soon as appropriate after the observation or reactions occur, thus keeping it concrete and relatively free of distortions that come with the lapse of time.

6. Focus feedback on the sharing of ideas and information rather than on giving advice.

By sharing ideas and information we leave the person free to decide for himself/herself, in the light of his/her own goals in a particular time, and how to use the ideas and the information. When we give advice we tell him/her what to do with the information, and in that sense we take away his/her freedom to determine for himself/herself what is for him/her the most appropriate course of action.

7. Focus feedback on exploration of alternatives rather than answers or solutions.

The more we can focus on a variety of procedures and means for the attainment of a particular goal, the less likely we are to accept prematurely a particular answer or solution-which may or may not fit our particular problem. Many of us go around with a collation of answers and solutions for which there are no problems.

8. Focus feedback on the value it may have to the recipient not on the value or release that it provides the person giving the feedback.

The feedback provided should serve the needs of the recipient rather than the needs of the giver. Help and feedback need to be given and heard as an offer, not an imposition.

9. Focus feedback on the amount of information that the person receiving it can use, rather than on the amount that you have which you might like to give.

To overload a person with feedback is to reduce the possibility that he/she may use what he/she receives effectively. When we give more than can be used we may be satisfying some need for ourselves rather than helping the other person.

10. Focus feedback on time and place so that personal data can be shared at appropriate times.

Because the reception and use of personal feedback involves many possible emotional reactions, it is important to be sensitive to when it is appropriate to provide feedback. Excellent feedback presented at an inappropriate time may do more harm than good.

11. Focus feedback on *what* is said rather than *why* it is said.

The aspects of feedback which relate to the what, how, when, where, of what is said are observable characteristics. The why of what is said takes us from the observable to the inferred, and brings up questions of *motive* or *intent*.

It may be helpful to think of *why* in terms of a specifiable goal or goals—which can then be considered in terms of time, place, procedures, probabilities of attainment, etc.

To make assumptions about the motives of the person giving the feedback may prevent us from hearing or cause us to distort what is said. In short, if I question "why" a person gives me feedback I may not hear what he says.

In short, the giving (and receiving) of feedback requires courage, skill, understanding, and respect for self and others.

THE EIGHT RULES OF FEEDBACK

Frederic H. Margolis

1. Feedback must be wanted or requested. It should be asked for, not imposed. It should be in the hands of the receiver, in that he/she asks for it and then controls how much of it he/she gets, its content and its depth.

2. Feedback is given for the benefit of the receiver. It is given to be helpful to the receiver, but does not obligate the receiver to change. The person who receives feedback can accept or reject the information and use it in the way he/she wishes.

3. Feedback is only the perception of the giver. It is neither right nor wrong. It only expresses his/her perception or feelings at the time it was given.

4. Since feedback is only the perception of the giver, both parties may wish to check with others who are present for their perceptions of the situation.

5. Feedback is more meaningful when it closely follows the event. It is very difficult to reconstruct situations when several days or even weeks have passed.

6. Feedback can be better understood and used when it is specific rather than general. To be told that one is *dominating* is not as useful as to be told that it is the specific behavior, such as talking and not listening, which makes the receiver seem that way.

7. Feedback will be received less defensively if it is descriptive rather than evaluative. To describe a person's behavior or to describe one's reaction to it, such as *I felt left out when you cut me off,* is more useful than *You always cut people off.*

8. Feedback should be useful and meaningful. It should be important enough to affect the receiver and directed toward behavior which can be changed. When feedback is too shallow, it is useless; when directed toward unchangeable behavior, it only leads to increased frustration.

Source: Frederic H. Margolis. (1970). *Training by objectives: a participant-oriented approach.* From Office of Economic Opportunity, June 1970, for Sterling Institute.

INDEPENDENT

LEARNING

and

LEARNING

CONTRACTS

SECTION TITLES

SOME GUIDELINES FOR USING LEARNING CONTRACTS
LEARNING CONTRACT

SOME GUIDELINES FOR USING LEARNING CONTRACTS

Malcolm S. Knowles

Why Use Learning Contracts?

One of the most significant findings from research about adult learning[1] is that when adults go about learning something naturally (as contrasted with being taught something), they are highly self-directing. Evidence is beginning to accumulate, too, that what adults learn on their own initiative they learn more deeply and permanently than what they learn by being taught.

Those kinds of learning that are engaged in for purely personal development can perhaps be planned and carried out completely by individuals on their own terms and with only a loose structure. But those kinds of learning that have as their purposes improving one's competence to perform in a job or in a profession must take into account the needs and expectations of the organizations, professions, and society. Learning contracts provide a means for negotiating a reconciliation between these external needs and expectations and the learner's internal needs and interests.

Furthermore, in traditional education the learning activity is structured by the teacher and the institution. The learners are told what objectives they are to work toward, what resources they are to use and how they are to use them, and how the accomplishment of the objectives will be evaluated. This imposed structure conflicts with the adult's deep psychological need to be self-directing and may induce resistance, apathy or withdrawal. Learning contracts provide a vehicle for making the planning of learning experiences a mutual undertaking between learners and their helpers, mentors, and often, peers. By participating in the process of diagnosing their learning needs, formulating their objectives, identifying resources, choosing learning strategies, and evaluating accomplishments, the learners develop a sense of ownership (and commitment to) the learning plan.

Finally, in learning through supervised field experiences especially, there is a strong possibility that what is to be learned from the experience will be less clear to both the learner and the field supervisor than what work is to be done. There is a long tradition of field-experience learners being exploited for the performance of menial tasks that the paid workers don't want to do. The learning contract is a means for making the learning objectives of the field experience clear and explicit for both the learner and the field supervisor.

---

[1] E.g., Allen Tough. (1979). *The Adult's Learning Projects.* Toronto: Ontario Institute for Studies in Education.

HOW DO YOU DEVELOP A LEARNING CONTRACT?

Step 1: Diagnose Your Learning Needs.

A learning need is the gap between where you are now and where you want to be in regard to a particular set of competencies.

You may already be aware of certain learning needs as a result of a personnel appraisal process or the long accumulation of evidence for yourself of the gaps between where you are now and where you would like to be.

If not, it might be worth your while to go through this process: First: construct a model of the competencies required to perform excellently the role (e.g. parent, teacher, civic leader, manager, consumer, professional worker, etc.) you are concerned about. There may be a competency model already in existence that you can use as a thought-starter and check-list; many vocations are developing such models. If not, you can build your own model; with the help of friends, colleagues, supervisors, and expert resource people. A competency can be thought of as the ability to do something at some level of proficiency, and is usually composed of some combination of knowledge, understandings, skills, attitudes, and values. For example, "ability to ride a bicycle from my home to the store" is a competency that involves some knowledge of how a bicycle operates and the route to the store; an understanding of some of the dangers inherent in riding a bicycle; skill in mounting, pedaling, steering, and stopping a bicycle; an attitude of desire to ride a bicycle; and a valuing of exercise it will yield. "Ability to ride a bicycle in a cross-country race" would be a higher-level competency that would require greater knowledge, understanding, skill, etc. It is useful to produce a competency model even if it is crude and subjective because of the clearer sense of direction it will give you.

Having constructed a competency model, your next task is to assess the gap between where you are now and where the model says you should be in regard to each competency. You can do this alone or with the help of people who have been observing your performance. The chances are that you will find that you have already developed some competencies to a level of excellence, so that you can concentrate on those that you haven't developed to that point.

Step 2: Specify Your Learning Objectives.

You are now ready to start filling out the first column of the learning contract. "Learning Objectives." Each of the learning needs diagnosed in Step 1 should be translated into a learning objective. Be sure that your objectives describe what you will learn, not what you will do to learn them (e.g. "To read five books" is not a learning objective but a strategy for using resources; the learning objective would describe what you want to learn by reading five books). State your objectives in whatever terms are most meaningful to you—content acquisition, terminal behaviors, or directions of growth.

Step 3: Specify Learning Resources and Strategies.

When you have finished listing your objectives, move over to the second column of the contract, "Learning Resources and Strategies," and describe how you propose to go about accomplishing each objective. Identify the resources (material and human) you plan to use and the strategies (techniques, tools) you will employ in making use of them. Here is an example:

LEARNING OBJECTIVE: To improve my ability to organize my work efficiently so that I can accomplish 20 percent more work in a day.

LEARNING RESOURCES AND STRATEGIES: (1) Find books and articles in the library on how to organize work and manage time and read them. (2) Interview three executives on how they organize their work, then observe them for one day each, noting techniques they use. (3) Select the best techniques from each, plan a day's work, and have a colleague observe me for a day, giving me feedback.

Step 4: Specify Evidence of Accomplishment.

After completing the second column in the contract form, move over to the third column, **Evidence of Accomplishment of Objectives**, and describe what evidence you will collect to indicate the degree to which you have achieved each objective. Perhaps the following examples of evidence for different types of objectives will stimulate your thinking about what evidence you might accumulate.

TYPE OF OBJECTIVE EXAMPLES OF EVIDENCE

Knowledge: Reports of knowledge acquired, as in essays, examinations, oral presentations, audio-visual presentations, annotated bibliographies, etc.

Understanding: Examples of utilization of knowledge in solving problems, as in action projects, research projects with conclusions and recommendations, program planning, organizational change proposals, etc.

Skills: Performance exercises, simulations, demonstrations, use of video-tapes of performance, etc.

Attitudes: Attitudinal rating scales, role playing, simulations exercises, critical incident cases, simulation exercises, etc.

Values: Value rating scales, performance in value clarification groups, critical incident cases, simulation exercises, etc.

Step 5: Specify How the Evidence Will Be Validated.

After you have specified what evidence you will collect for each objective in column three, move over to column four, "Criteria and Means for Validating Evidence." For each objective, first specify the criteria by which the evidence is to be judged. The criteria will vary according to the type of objective. For example, criteria for knowledge objectives might include depth, comprehensiveness, precision, clarity, accuracy, usefulness, scholarliness, etc. For skill objectives the criteria might include poise, speed, precision, flexibility, gracefulness, style, imaginativeness, etc. For attitudes and values they might be consistency, immediacy of action, confidence in action, etc. After you have specified the criteria, indicate the means you propose to use to have the evidence judged according to these criteria. For example, if you produce a paper or report as evidence of accomplishment of a knowledge objective, whom will you have read it and what are their qualifications? Will they express their judgment by rating scales, descriptive reports, evaluative reports, or how? If you are getting a rating of your accomplishment of a skill objective, whom will you have observe you performing the skill—students, peers, experts: and what kind of feedback about your performance will you ask them to give you? One of the actions that helps to differentiate distinguished from adequate performance in self-directed learning is the wisdom with which a learner selects his or her validators.

Step 6: Review Your Contract With Consultants.

After you have completed the first draft of your contract, you will find it useful to review it with two or three friends, supervisors, or other consultants to get their reactions and suggestions. Here are some questions you might ask them to react to.

- Are the learning objectives clear, understandable, and realistic: and do they describe accurately what you propose to learn?

- Can they think of other objectives you might consider?

- Do the learning strategies and resources seem reasonable, appropriate, and efficient? Can they suggest other resources?

- Does the evidence seem relevant to the various objectives, and would it convince them? Can they think of other evidence you might consider?

- Are the criteria and means for validating the evidence clear, relevant, and convincing? Can they think of other evidence that you might consider?

Step 7: Carry Out the Contract.

You now simply do what the contract calls for. But keep in mind that as you work on it you may find that your notions about what you want to learn and how you want to learn it may change. So don't hesitate to revise your contract as you go along.

Step 8: Evaluate Your Learning.

When you have completed your contract you will want to get some assurance that you have in fact learned what you set out to learn. Perhaps the simplest way to do this is to ask the consultants you used in Step 6 to examine your evidence and validation data and give you their judgment about their adequacy.

LEARNING CONTRACT

© Malcolm S. Knowles

Learner _____

Learning Experience _____

What are you going to learn?	How are you going to learn it (resources and strategy)?	Target date for completion	How are you going to know that you learned it (evidence)?	How are you going to prove that you learned it (verification by experts/professionals)?

EVALUATION
of
TRAINING

SECTION TITLES

EVALUATION OF TRAINING
EVALUATION OF INSTRUCTIONAL PROGRAMS
VARIATIONS ON THE EVALUATION PROCESS
SIMPLE TRAINEE REACTION FORM

EVALUATION OF TRAINING

L. Robert Kohls

1. Planned before training begins (i.e. in design stage) as part of total training design

2. Keyed to behavioral objectives of the course (Evaluation then becomes merely determining whether the stated objectives have been met, or how well they have been met)

3. Should be as unobtrusive as possible

4. Findings of evaluation produce changes indicated in next iteration of course (= feedback loop)

5. Four needs for evaluation in training process:

    a. Needs Assessment—established whether there is a need for training; whether training can be expected to solve the problem

    b. Input Evaluation—establishes state of knowledge of incoming (i.e. untrained) trainees

    c. Process Evaluation—monitors ongoing training sessions

    d. Product Evaluation—measures impact of the training on the trainees (i.e. changes due to the training)

6. Four elements which can be evaluated:

    a. Reaction (of the trainees)

    b. Learning

    c. Behavior Change

    d. Results (e.g., reduced costs, improved operation, increase in quantity etc.)

7. Evaluation phases:

    a. Pre-training

    b. Post-training

    c. Follow-up

8. Some accepted measurement methods:

    a. Observation

    b. Ratings (by independent raters)

    c. Trainee surveys

    d. Trainee interviews

    e. Instructor interviews

    f. Supervisor surveys

    g. Supervisor interviews

EVALUATION OF INSTRUCTIONAL PROGRAMS

Paul A. Friesen

According to the systematic approach we have been discussing, the development of an instructional program is initiated because a particular need has been identified. In turn, the development of any form of evaluation of that instruction should take place in conjunction with the design of that program.

Instructional programs are evaluated to determine whether or not they have fulfilled their objectives. Thus, the first important step in evaluation is to ensure that the instructional objectives are precisely defined, in behavioral terms, so that the results are observable and measurable. If the objectives are vague, ambivalent or even non-existent, there is no way that the designer can decide whether or not the program has done its job.

A second important point to remember before even beginning to think of an evaluation process is learner selection. In order to validly determine if the instruction is meeting the needs of the learners as well as meeting the instructional objectives, he must first ensure that the people selected are the ones for whom the instruction was intended. The best possible program will not achieve its objectives when given to the *wrong* population.

Thirdly, the designer must be able to clearly state the purpose of evaluation. That is, there should not be evaluation for its own sake, as a token response from the designer, nor as an ego-boosting *joy sheet* for him at the end of a good session. If the program did not meet its objectives, the evaluation should be able to indicate the areas in which he should make improvements and changes. Also, in line with this, feedback on the evaluation should be given to all concerned, including the participants, their supervisors, if any, and interested management groups if this is training in an organization.

In discussing evaluation of instructional programs, let us assume that the instruction is for people who will be going to a post-training situation with a supervisor who will know how effectively they are working.

Areas To Be Evaluated

There are three basic areas around which an evaluation pattern can develop:

1. **Trainee Progress**: Is there a significant pre-post-training difference in the job behavior of the trainee in terms of objectives, of the instructional program? Is this change sustained or does it last only a few days or weeks after the training is completed?

2. **Training Program**: Does it meet organization needs? Are its objectives really aligned with organization objectives, policies, and structure? In conjunction with this, is the training population the most appropriate for this program?

3. **Trainers, Methods, Techniques, Materials**: Were the trainers competent? Qualified? Were the methods, techniques and materials appropriate and effective?

What type of evaluation will provide the answers to questions in all three areas? Let's look briefly at the following two sections and then try to put it all together in an evaluation pattern.

Source: Paul A. Friesen. (1971). *Designing instruction.* Ottawa, Ontario: Friesen, Kaye and Associates, Ltd. Used by permission of Friesen, Kaye and Associates, Ltd., an international training and consulting firm specializing in Train-the-Trainer workshops and a full course design and development service.

Phases of Evaluation

An effective evaluation of an instructional program can be done in three phases:

1. **Pre-Training**: This includes some type of questionnaire or interview to determine the expectations of the prospective learners and their supervisors. What do they see as the objectives of the training? How will the instruction fit into career development plans? What were the criteria for selection of each nominee?

2. **Post-Training**: Do the trainers feel that the program was all it was purposed to be? Were their individual needs fulfilled? What changes would they like to see? Can they now give examples of situations in which they will be able to apply this training? Can the supervisors see how this training will be applied? These questions should be asked immediately after the instructional program is completed.

3. **Follow-up**: This stage of the evaluation could take place a few weeks, months or even a year after the actual instruction. It could also be done periodically, for example, once a month for six months, depending on the course content, the purpose of the evaluation, etc.

Levels of Evaluation

There are three types of personnel who should do evaluation:

Trainee: Was the training what he expected? What he needed? Were his expectations fulfilled? Did he know why he was nominated or why he chose to take the training? How is he using the training?

Supervisors: Why was this trainee chosen to take this particular training? How will it help him? Were the objectives of the program and its usefulness discussed with the subordinate? Did the training help the employee? Does the employee use the training? Effectively?

Trainer: A trainer is usually his own most harsh critic and, as such, he should not only do his own evaluation of the training but also use the evaluation of the trainees and their supervisors to improve the course, if necessary.

A Pattern of Evaluation

We can now see what has to be evaluated, when and by whom. How can we put this together so that we have an overall smoothly-flowing evaluation pattern?

The following chart should help put all this in perspective. The skeleton of the chart looks like this:

	Pattern For Evaluation	
	PRE-TRAINING	
TRAINEE		**SUPERVISOR**
	POST TRAINING	
TRAINEE		**SUPERVISOR**
	FOLLOW-UP	
TRAINEE		**SUPERVISOR**

For our purpose, we will break the chart into three sections—*Pre-training, Post-training and Follow-up*—discussing each section in turn.

The trainer's role will be outlined after each section as he, naturally, has to do somewhat more than answer questions. The trainer is the designer, collector and consumer of the evaluation data. He not only has to obtain answers to certain questions, but must use those answers effectively as possible in terms of the objectives of the program, the organization and the trainees.

Pre-training Evaluation

Pre-Training

Trainees	Supervisors
1. What do you think are the specific objectives of the training?	1. What do you think are the specific objectives of the training?
2. How do you see this training fitting into your own career path?	2. How do you see this training fitting into the career plans of your subordinate?
3. Have you discussed this training with your supervisor? If so, are your expectations the same or different?	3. Have you discussed the training with your supervisor? If so, are your expectations the same or different?
4. As far as you know, who participated in deciding that you should have this training?	4. Who else participated in deciding that your subordinate needed this training?
5. Can you list examples of situations during the past half year that would indicate to you a need for this training?	5. Can you list examples of situations during the past half year that would indicate to you a need for your subordinate to have this training?

The above questions can form the basis of a questionnaire to be sent to the nominated trainees and their supervisors at least a few weeks before the training is to start.

Some of the answers might indicate that more groundwork should have been laid or that, possibly, the most appropriate trainees have not been chosen.

What is the trainer's role? He has asked these questions. What does he do with the answers?

Let's assume that the specific objectives of the training, as seen by the trainees and supervisors, are not the ones that the trainer listed. Obviously, there has been a lack of true communication or a miscommunication. When the trainee was told that he would be involved in some type of training, whether he was nominated or volunteered, he should have been told the exact purpose of the training. This is something that the supervisor should also know.

There are several situations which could give rise to faulty communication. For example:

1. Neither the supervisor nor the trainee was informed of the objectives of the training. As too often happens, it may have been a case of a phone call or a memo from the training section saying, in effect, *Joe, you're going on a supervisor's training course in two weeks. We are enclosing some material for you to work on before you come.* In this case, the trainee has to make sure that his supervisor knows. Believe it or not, sometimes, he has not been told.

2.   Another common situation is that the supervisor has received a memorandum saying that Joe is going on this supervisor's course in two weeks and will the supervisor please discuss the course with Joe and help prepare him for it. Unfortunately, the supervisor does not have the time, or does not consider it important to discuss the objectives of the course with Joe, even though they are stated quite clearly. After all, a supervisors' course tells how to be a supervisor and Joe will find out the details when he gets there! Hogwash!

These types of situations arise with regard to expectations of the trainee and his supervisor. Even if the supervisor had his subordinate review the objectives of the training, they might not discuss them in terms of their expectations when Joe comes back to his job or in terms of furthering Joe's career.

Ideally, the supervisor, armed with a training outline and a knowledge of Joe's abilities and aspirations, and of the organization's needs, should nominate him for a particular training course. He should know what Joe has been doing, what he is capable of doing and what the organization needs done.

Then, if it is confirmed (by the training section, the manpower planning section or whatever department has authority for approval) that Joe is, indeed, going to receive that training, the trainer has certain responsibilities. He should formally advise both Joe and his supervisor that Joe is expected on the course, outline the objectives of the course, and request that they discuss them together in terms of their expectations.

At this point, the trainer would also request that both Joe and his supervisor complete the pre-training questionnaire or, if this is to be done by interview, that an appointment be made.

This type of evaluation is usually done in the form of a written questionnaire, since interviews are often too lengthy and costly to be justified to management.

As well as general questions listed above, the trainer could list specific components of the course as it has been designed, and ask the trainee and his supervisor for comments on the need for and applicability of training in those areas.

By now the trainer has asked his questions, received answers and, hopefully, done something with them. As the training program should already have been tested, the most common *somethings* which would be done at this point would probably be to reconsider the selection of a trainee or to rectify a faulty communication.

Post-training Evaluation

The training is now completed. It may have lasted two days, two weeks or extended over a year. No matter what the duration, the evaluation pattern remains the same:

Post-Training

Trainees	Supervisors
1. Have any of your ideas changed about the objectives of this training?	1. Have you discussed the training course with your subordinate? In detail? With what results?
2. List examples of situations on the job in which use can be made of what you learned during this training session.	2. Have any of your ideas changed about the objectives of this training? If so, in what way?
3. What situations during the past half year might you have handled differently if you had already taken this training? Do you think the outcome would have been different? Give examples.	3. What are your plans to follow-up on your subordinates use of what he learned from the training?
4. What plans do you have for discussing this training session with your supervisor?	4. Other comments?

If possible, the trainer's questionnaire should be completed at the very end of the training session. This ensures the greatest number of responses. All too often, if the trainer asks that the questionnaire be mailed in a few days, he never sees it again. Of course, that might be taken as an evaluation itself!

The supervisor's questionnaire should be sent out in time for the supervisor to complete it in the first one or two days that the subordinate is back on the job.

As well as the general questions listed above, the trainer, as in the pre-training questionnaire, might well use a specific breakdown into the various components of the training and ask for comments on their usefulness and applicability.

The answers to questions on the objectives and usefulness of the training in job situations should be compared with the answers received from the pre-training questionnaire.

If you feel it necessary to link the two questionnaires on a one-to-one basis rather than a general statement of the overall results, it would probably be more effective to ask that the questionnaire be coded numerically rather than by actual names of the trainees. A sense of anonymity often ensures a more frank response, especially if the trainees have to go to any trouble to mail or deliver their responses.

Usually, unless the instruction itself has been poor, or if the designer has not followed a systematic procedure, the post-training evaluation will generally be fairly favorable; that is, the trainees will say that the training was good. But, those same people may give quite a different answer in a few weeks or months.

Follow-Up Evaluation

Follow-Up

Trainees	Supervisors
1. Have you used any of the concepts and methods learned in the training session on your job? If so, give specific examples.	1. Has your subordinate discussed any of the concepts and methods he learned in the training session with regard to his actual job? If so, give examples.
2. Were there times when you tried to use some of these concepts and methods and found they were not useful? If so, give specific examples.	2. Have you been able to follow-up on his use of any of the concepts and methods? If yes, give specific examples?
3. If you have not been able to apply the training, what do you consider to be the reason?	3. If your subordinate has not been able to apply his training, what do you consider to be the reasons?

As with the other questionnaires, the trainer could be specific about the various training components in his wording of some of the above questions.

The follow-up evaluation questionnaire should not be sent to the trainees and their supervisors until there has been sufficient time for the trainees to use what was learned in the training course. This may require only a few days or it may take several months, depending on content, procedures, etc.

For some types of training, the trainer may wish to evaluate the effectiveness of the training several times in the following year. For example, emergency procedures for flight attendants might rarely be used, but a test of the retention of the knowledge of those procedures should probably be carried out periodically.

The trainer has asked more questions and has received more answers. He must do something with them. For example, if the trainee has not retained the concept of delegation and its applicability in his job as a supervisor, maybe there should be more practice and exercise in that area during the course.

If the trainee and/or his supervisor state reasons for the trainee not using what he learned, it is possible that the trainer should re-assess the process by which selection of the trainees was made, or the need for that particular training.

The pattern of evaluation that the trainer develops should be based on some kind of continuum so that the questions asked in each of the three phases can be related and action taken on the responses.

Types of Evaluation

Quantified: the questions can be weighted. A simple example is a 5 or 9 point rating scale on which the respondent rates the usefulness of each component of the training program. This is the most simple system of evaluating an instructional program. However, in the next section of this text, there will be a detailed discussion of program validation.

Unquantified: More detailed information can be elicited when open-ended questions are used. This gives the respondents an opportunity to express their own opinions on various techniques, methods, and trainers and on the appropriateness and effectiveness of the content. This method is more time-consuming for the trainer as the responses must be carefully sifted and weighed.

A combination of both **quantified** and **unquantified** evaluation is sometimes appropriate. For example, on a Follow-up questionnaire after a supervisory training course:

E.g. We are asking you to consider the subject areas that were covered in the Supervisory Course, in terms of their applicability to your day to day work. If possible, we would like you to give us examples of how you might have used some of these concepts and methods in the last few months.

Would you also note any situations where you tried these concepts and methods and did not find them helpful?

1. Managing Time?

1	2	3	4	5	6	7	8	9
Useless		Of Some Use		Useful		Very Useful		Extremely Useful

Examples:

_____

_____

_____

Use of Evaluation

All too often people complain that they seem to be filling in endless numbers of questionnaires without knowing why, or what happens to the results. The frequent poor response to post-training and follow-up evaluation questionnaires is perhaps indicative of this attitude based on a lack of feedback. The respondents should be told the purpose of the evaluation questionnaire and should be given feedback, such as a summary of responses and an indication of proposed changes based on those responses. The percentage of questionnaires returned will likely increase when the respondents, both trainees and supervisors, are aware that something is being done and their effort and time were well spent.

Summary

Coping with instructional evaluation is not easy. Indeed, it is often so complex and time-consuming that instructional designers simply ignore it in the hope that it will go away. That this attitude is not acceptable if we are to achieve the most effective and efficient instruction possible should be obvious by now. Moreover, it is often a very traumatic experience for the designer to learn that his baby just isn't up to scratch, and facing that reality is hard on the ego. Yet, without careful evaluation, no definitive answers to why it failed or succeeded can be secured. Hence we must evaluate—and carefully.

Variations on the Evaluation Process

L. Robert Kohls and John M. Knight

Several more creative approaches to evaluation may challenge both the facilitator and the participants.

One approach is something like this:

> Before the workshop begins, the facilitator should hand-pick three partici-
> pants who have the background, experience and maturity (but who do not
> necessarily have prior content knowledge of the subject) and give them the
> assignment of evaluating the workshop. They need be given no further in-
> structions, other than to evaluate the facilitator(s), the exercises, and the
> workshop's attainment of the stated objectives. So long as they achieve
> these ends, they may do the job in any way they decide.

Several other nontraditional approaches are outlined in the March 1980 issue of the *Bulletin on Training*. These include:

- Dividing the total workshop group into three equal teams and assigning each team the task of suggesting ways to improve one of the following aspects of the work-shop: the course content, the methodology, or the logistical arrangements. Each of these small groups should then report orally to the whole group, while someone captures all the comments on a flip chart.

- Dividing the group into pairs or triads and assigning each of these subgroups the task of coming up with two things that were especially memorable in the workshop or two suggestions for improving the workshop. These ideas should then be shared with the whole group while someone captures all the comments on a flip chart.

- Forming a circle and having participants tell one thing they have learned from the course, allowing other members of the group to add comments as each point is made. These comments also should be captured on a flip chart. Ask participants what new perspectives they have gained as a result of the workshop. Have their atti-tudes changed, and if so, in what ways?

Source: L. Robert Kohls and John M. Knight. (1994). *Developing intercultural aware-ness*. Yarmouth, ME: Intercultural Press.

SIMPLE TRAINEE REACTION FORM

Alan Kotok

Please answer the following few questions so we can learn your reactions to this seminar and help us prepare future programs of this type. Most questions require only an "X" in the appropriate space. You need not sign your name. Thanks for your help.

How would you rate this program overall?

❑ Excellent

❑ Good

❑ Only fair

❑ Poor

Did this program meet:

❑ All of your expectations

❑ Most of your expectations

❑ Some of your expectations

❑ None of your expectations

In your opinion, did the program contain:

❑ Too much material for the time allotted

❑ About the right amount of material

❑ Not enough material—too many sessions dragged

How would you rate the administration of this program:

❑ Excellent—The program ran smoothly from start to finish

❑ Good—Most aspects of the program ran smoothly

❑ Fair—Only a few aspects of the program ran smoothly

❑ Poor—No aspects of the program ran smoothly

Which sessions of this program (if any) did you consider particularly useful or informative?

Please list no more than two or three. You may consult your program schedules if you wish.

And which sessions of this program (if any) did you consider particularly uninformative?

Please list no more than *two or three*. Again, you can consult your schedules, if you wish.

What should be done to improve this program in the future?

APPENDICES:

TRAINING
WORKSHOP
DESIGN

SECTION TITLES

UNDERSTANDING AND WORKING WITH ADULT LEARNERS

MASTER TRAINER DEMONSTRATIONS

TRAINING METHODOLOGIES FOR DEVELOPING INTERCULTURAL SKILLS (A SEMESTER-LONG, THREE-CREDIT UNIVERSITY COURSE)

UNDERSTANDING AND WORKING WITH ADULT LEARNERS
Malcolm S. Knowles

Workshop

Competency-Development Objectives

1. An understanding of the modern concepts of adult learning and how these differ from traditional concepts of youth learning.
2. An understanding of the role of educator as facilitator and resource for self-directed learners.
3. The ability to apply these concepts to the designing of learning experiences for one's self and others through the use of learning contracts.

Schedule

9:00-10:00 a.m. Climate setting exercise. Sharing of information in small groups about participants' whats, whos, and questions, problems, or issues.

10:00-10:15 a.m. Analysis of this experience and identification of the characteristics of a climate that is conducive to learning.

10:15-10:30 a.m. Break.

10:30-11:30 a.m. Dialogic presentation of the theoretical framework for andragogy.

11:30-12:00 noon. Introduction to competency-based education and a model of competencies for facilitators of learning.

12:00-1:00 p.m. Lunch.

1:00-1:30 p.m. Diagnosis of competency-development needs by participants.

1:30-2:30 p.m. Drafting of learning contracts.

Introduction to Contract Learning
Individuals draft contracts for their two or three highest priority
learning objectives
Individuals review contracts in triads

2:30-2:45 p.m. Break.

2:45-3:30 p.m. Problem clinic. Response to questions about this and any unresolved problems and issues.

3:30-4:00 p.m. Evaluation of this workshop.

4:00 p.m. Adjourn.

MASTER TRAINER DEMONSTRATIONS

L. Robert Kohls

1.	Case Studies	Three Intercultural Training Situations (to compare, analyze, and determine *Training Needs*.)
2.	Case Studies	Interrelated, *Progressive* Cases.
3.	Short Case Studies	Around situations involving a foreign student on an American campus (seen from the point of view of the foreign student).
4.	Leading Discussions	Based on Provocative Materials (*Chinese Editor's Rejection Slip* and Khomeni Article).
5.	Leading Discussions	Based on an Article (*Inductive Methods for Deductive Minds*).
6.	Leading Discussions	Based on a Videotape/Film (*American Social Behavior*).
7.	Interactive Use of Overhead Projector	Discovering America's Implicit Cultural Assumptions.
8.	Role Plays	With Mr. Khan and a *real* Mr. Smith (selected contrast person); using exhaustive Processing Techniques.
9.	Role Plays	With Mr. Khan and WIC Trainers playing Mr./Ms. Smith.
10.	Role Plays	Using scenarios created by WIC Trainers (Taped by Port-a-Pak and replayed for immediate feedback and critique).
11.	Role Plays	In Triads, using Role Plays and *Guidelines to Cross-Cultural Communications* created by Norma McCaig (with observer to critique, based on *Guidelines*).
12.	Leading Exercises	Agree-Disagree Statements (and processing).
13.	Leading Exercises	*Buzz Groups* (with reporting back to whole group).
14.	Leading Exercises	Discovering American Values through American Proverbs (plus Creating New Proverbs around specified values).
15.	Small Group Exercises	Breakout Groups (Dyads, Triads, Buzz Groups); Personal experiences regarding Culture Shock and Return Culture Shock (and flip chart processing).
16.	Small Group Exercises	Value Option Cards with several related exercises.
17.	Orchestrated Debate	Defending an Alien Proposal.
18.	Open Discussion	To determine where we go from here...

Presented by L. Robert Kohls for Staff Development at the Washington International Center of Meridian House International, Washington, D.C.

TRAINING METHODOLOGIES FOR DEVELOPING INTERCULTURAL SKILLS

(A Semester-long, Three-credit University Course)
L. Robert Kohls

Description
This course introduces students to the broad array of training methodologies—ranging from small group discussions to case studies, role plays, games and simulations—which are available to the intercultural trainer for use in developing intercultural awareness in a culturally naive audience. The class will be led through all these activities by an experienced trainer-professor. Although this class would be most helpful in preparing people to become intercultural trainers themselves, no single three-unit course can hope to achieve this end.

Goals
1. To examine the full range of instructional techniques currently used in training and development
2. To understand the relationship between the content/purpose of the training session and the specific training activities which are most appropriate to delivering that content and purpose
3. To experience the broadest possible range of intercultural training methodologies

Objectives
Each student who successfully completes this course will be able to:
1. Assess areas of personal strengths and establish goals for further developing his/her training skills
2. Identify assumptions of how adults learn, and how these assumptions influence the selection of intercultural methodologies
3. Select appropriate training activities according to participant need and planned content of the training program or session
4. Plan a training session based on need and content
5. Demonstrate a practical knowledge of a variety of instructional methods, using the experiential learning model

Outline

Week 1:	Self Introductions Course Description and Housekeeping Details Review of Expectation of Students The TRAINING CONTEXT *Training* compared with *Education*
Readings:	K-T: I -3/4-13/14-19/20/21/23/24, 25/26/33, 34

Week 2:	Components of Training: 1. Training Technology 2. Training Methodologies 3. Platform Skills [This course focuses only on the second area.]
Readings:	K-T: 53/52/68-70/50, 51 S & D: 3-6
Week 3:	Characteristics of Adult Learners Comparative Learning Theories Inductive cf. Deductive Pedagogy cf. Andragogy Experiential Learning
Readings:	K-T: 40 S & D: 9-12/14, 15/17, 18 JE: 16-18

Week 4:	Determining Training Needs and Assessing the Audience;
	    Heterogeneity of Virtually Every Training Group
	Dealing with Dysfunctional Group Behaviors;
	    Handling Training Problems

Readings:	K-T: 45-49/54 S & D: 63-66/68 JE: 268-270/277, 278

Week 5:	Realistic Expectations of What Training Can Accomplish;
	    Anatomy of a Trainer—ASTD Competencies
	Experiential Training Model
	    Instructional Systems Design (ISD)
	    Anatomy of a Training Session
	Specific Training Goals
	    To Impart KNOWLEDGE
	    To Change ATTITUDES
	    To Develop SKILLS

Readings:	K-T: 27-32/36/41, 42/64/65-67/71 S & D: 83-95 JE: 110-115/272-277
Week 6:	An Overview of Training Methodologies (from "Cool" to "Hot") Pros and Cons of Each Methodology Selection of Method/Activity According to Need and for Variety Sequencing of Activities
Readings:	K-T: 68-70/71/23 S & D: 23-47 JE: 270-272

Week 7:	Ice-Breakers Lectures/Lecturettes Audio-Visual Support Systems
Readings:	Sue Forbes-Greene: *The Encyclopedia of Icebreakers,* (San Diego: Applied Skills Press, 1983.) JE: 2-9/232-244 S & D: 169-171/201-240 K-M: 10, 11/62-78

Week 8:	Breakout Groups
	   Buzz Groups
	   Dyads/Triads
	   Size of Group Conditions the Results

Readings:	K-M: 25/35, 36/31-35 JE: 20-31
Week 9:	Agree-Disagree Statements Leading Group Discussions Structured Exercises and Small Group Activities
Readings:	S & D: 151-153/159-161 K-M: 23-25/28-31 K-D: 3, 4/5, 6/7-11/13/64 JE: 10-19/32-52/89-100/116-127
Week 10:	Training Videos Training Films Videotaping, Playback, and Critique
Readings:	JE: 197-208 K-D: 70-73 K-M: 85, 86
Week 11:	Question-and-Answer Sessions Interviewing an Expert Panel of Experts
Readings:	K-M: 13/20, 21/14-16
Week 12:	Case Studies/Critical Incidents
Readings:	JE: 209-231 K-M: 37-40 S & D: 182, 183 K-D: 18-26/27-63 Richard Brislin et al.: *International Interactions: A Practical Guide.* (Beverly Hills: Sage Publications, 1986)
Week 13:	Role Play
Readings:	JE: 53-76 K-M: 45-48 S & D: 183-186

Week 14:	Games
	Simulations
Readings:	JE: 77-88
	K-M: 50-55
	K-D: 15-17
Week 15:	Related Skills:
	Group Facilitation
	Feedback
	Learning Objectives
	On-the-Job Training
	Job Aids Checklist
	Evaluation
	Follow-Up Activities to Reinforce Learning
	Critique of This Course (Feedback to Instructor)
Readings:	K-T: 37-39/72-74/75/58-61 /62/76, 77/78-84/85-86
	JE: 245-253/254-265
	S & D: 73-75/78/102, 103/117-120/122/141-144/146, 147
	K-M: 60, 61/79-88
	K-D: 73-76

Instructional Methods

Students will experience all of the (more than 20) methodologies listed under Weeks 7 through 14 (above).

Grading and Evaluation

Midterm

Final Examination

Participant-Observer's Journal

Class Participation

Reading Assignments

Reading assignments are given in page numbers. The alphabetical indicators refer to the following code:

JE—Julius E. Eitington: *The Winning Trainer.*

K-D—L. Robert Kohls: *Developing Intercultural Awareness.*

K-M—L. Robert Kohls: *Methodologies for Trainers: A Compendium of Learning Strategies.*

K-T—L. Robert Kohls: *Training Know-How for Cross-Cultural Trainers.*

S & D—Barry J. Smith and Brian L. Delahaye: *How to Be an Effective Trainer.*

TRAINING

BIBLIOGRAPHY

SECTION TITLES

BIBLIOGRAPHY
INDEX

BIBLIOGRAPHY

Compiled by
David C. Wigglesworth, Ph.D.

Apps, Jerold. (1991). *Mastering the teaching of adults.* Melbourne, FL: Krieger.

Batchelder, D., and E. Warner. (1977). *Beyond experience: the experiential approach to cross-cultural education.* Brattleboro, VT: The Experiment Press.

Ben-Yoseph, Miriam. (1988). *Designing and delivering cross-cultural instruction.* Ypsilanti, MI: Eastern Michigan University Report.

Bennett, Milton J. (1986). A development approach to training for intercultural sensitivity. *International Journal of Intercultural Relations* 10, 179-196.

Black, J. Stewart, and Mark Mendenhall. (1989). A practical but theory-based framework for selecting cross-cultural training methods. *Human Resource Management,* Winter 1989.

Black, J. Stewart, and Mark Mendenhall. (1990). Cross-cultural training effectiveness: a review and a theoretical framework for future research. *Academy of Management Review,* Vol. 15.

Boulding, Elise. (1990). *Building a global civic culture: education for an independent world.* Syracuse, NY: Syracuse University Press.

Briggs, L. (1977). *Instructional design: principles and applications.* Englewood Cliffs, NJ: Educational Technology Publications (Prentice-Hall).

Brislin, Richard. (1990). *Applied cross-cultural research.* Thousand Oaks, CA: Sage.

Carbaugh, Donald (Ed.). (1990). *Cultural communication and intercultural contact.* Hillsdale, NJ: L. Erlbasum Associates.

Cassara, Beverly (Ed.). (1993). *Adult education in a multicultural society.* New York, NY: Routlege.

Casse, Pierre. (1979). *Training for the cross-cultural mind.* Washington, DC: Society for Intercultural Education, Training, and Research (SIETAR).

Casse, Pierre. (1982). *Training for the multicultural manager.* Washington, DC: Society for Intercultural Education, Training, and Research (SIETAR).

Conference Board. (1990). *Building global teamwork for growth and survival.* New York, NY: The Conference Board Research Bulletin No. 228.

Craig, Robert. (1987). *Training and development handbook: a guide to human resource development.* New York: McGraw-Hill.

Dodd, Carley. (1991). *Dynamics of intercultural communication* (3rd Edition). Dubuque, IA: William C. Brown.

Dyer, Wayne. (1977). *Team building: issues and alternatives.* Reading, MA: Addison-Wesley.

Eitington, Julius E. (1984). *The winning trainer.* Baltimore, MD: American Society for Training and Development.

Fitz-enz, Jac. (1990). *Human value management.* San Francisco, CA: Jossey-Bass.

Fowler, Sandra M., and Monica Mumford. (1995). *Intercultural sourcebook.* Yarmouth, ME: Intercultural Press.

Gagne, R., and L. Briggs. (1979). *Principles of instructional design.* New York, NY: Holt, Rinehart and Winston.

Gardenswartz, Lee, and Anita Rowe. (1994). *Managing diversity: a complete desk reference and planning guide.* Fredonia, NY: H. R. Press.

Gayeski, Dianne, Ed Nathan and Jon Sickle. (1992). Creating a CBT system for multinational training. *Interactive Learning International,* January-March 1992.

Grove Consultants International. (1994). *Effective facilitation: achieving results with groups.* San Francisco: Grove Consultants International.

Harris, Philip, and Robert Moran. (1990). *Managing cultural differences.* Houston, TX: Gulf Publishing.

Harrison, Roger, and Richard L. Hopkins. (1967). The design of cross-cultural training: an alternative to the university model. *Journal of Applied Behavioral Sciences* III, 4.

Hemphill, David. (1992). Thinking hard about culture in adult education: not a trivial pursuit. *Adult Learning.* May 1992.

Hoopes, David, and Paul Ventura (Eds.). (1979). *Intercultural sourcebook: cross-cultural training methodologies.* Yarmouth, ME: Intercultural Press.

Johnson, Philip. (1991). Transcending cultural differences through experiential teaching techniques. *Adult Learning.* November 1991.

Kirkpatrick, Donald L. (1994). *Evaluating training programs: the four levels.* San Francisco, CA: Berrett-Koehler Publishers.

Knowles, Malcolm S. (1975). *Self-directed learning: a guide for learners and teachers.* Chicago, IL: Association Press/Follet.

Knowles, Malcolm S. (1978). *The adult learner, a neglected species.* Houston, TX: Gulf Publishing Company.

Knowles, Malcolm S. (1980). *The modern practice of adult education: from pedagogy to andragogy.* Chicago, IL: Chicago Association Press/Follet.

Knowles, Malcolm S. (1984). *Andragogy in action: applying modern principles of adult learning.* San Francisco, CA: Jossey-Bass.

Knowles, Malcolm S. (1986). *Using learning contracts: practical approaches to individualizing and structuring learning.* San Francisco, CA: Jossey-Bass.

Knox, A. (1977). *Adult development and learning.* San Francisco, CA: Jossey-Bass.

Kohls, L. Robert. (1979). *Methodologies for trainers: a compendium of learning strategies.* Washington, DC: Future Life Press.

Kohls, L. Robert. (1995). *Survival kit for overseas living.* Yarmouth, ME: Intercultural Press.

Kohls, L. Robert, and John M. Knight. (1994). *Developing intercultural awareness.* Yarmouth, ME: Intercultural Press.

Kohls, L. Robert, and V. Lynn Tyler. (1989). *A select guide to area studies resources.* Provo, UT: Brigham Young University Press.

Laird, Duncan. (1985). *Approaches to training and development.* Reading, MA: Addison-Wesley.

Landis, Donald, and Richard Brislin. (1983). *Handbook of intercultural training* (3 volumes). New York, NY: Pergamon Press.

Lineberry, C., and D. Bullock. (1980). *Job Aids.* Volume 25 in *The Instructional Design Library.* Englewood Cliffs, NJ: Educational Technology Publications (Prentice-Hall).

Lovell, A. B. (1980). *Adult Learning.* London: Croan Helm.

Lynch, James. (1989). *Multicultural education: a global approach.* Washington, DC: Taylor & Francis.

Mager, Robert F. (1975). *Preparing instructional objectives.* Palo Alto, CA: Fearon Publishers.

Mager, Robert F. (1988). *Making instruction work.* Belmont, CA: Davis S. Lake.

Margolis, Frederick H., and Chip Bell. (1986). *Instructing for results.* San Diego, CA: University Associates.

Marquardt, Michael, and Dean Engel. (1993). *Global human resource development.* Englewood Cliffs, NJ: Prentice-Hall.

McLagan, Patricia. (1989). *Models for HRD Practice.* (4 vols). Alexandria, VA: American Society for Training and Development.

Middleton, John. (1991). *Vocational and technical education and training: a World Bank policy paper.* ERIC Document No. ED334454. A report by the International Bank for Reconstruction and Development.

Moricol, Keith, and Benhong Tsai. (1992). Adapting training for other cultures. *Training & Development Magazine.* April 1992.

Murray, Margo et al. (Eds.). (1992). The 1992 global connector: the complete resource directory for international training and development. *Annual Directory of International Training Associations, Institutions, Societies, and Training and Consulting Firms.*

Nadler, Leonard. (1984). *The handbook of human resource development.* New York, NY: John Wiley.

Nadler, Leonard. (1985). *The trainer's resource.* Alexandria, VA: American Association for Counseling and Development.

Nilson, Carolyn. (1989). *Training program workbook and kit.* Englewood Cliffs, NJ: Prentice Hall.

Nilson, Carolyn. (1990). *Training for non-trainers: a do-it-yourself guide for managers.* New York: AMACOM.

Nilson, Carolyn. (1991). *How to manage training.* New York, NY: AMACOM.

Odenwald, Sylvia. (1993). *Global training: how to design a program for a multinational corporation.* Burr Ridge, IL: Irwin Professional Publishing.

O'Hara-Devereaux, Mary, and Robert Johansen. (1994). *GlobalWork: bridging distance, culture and time.* San Francisco: Jossey-Bass Publishers.

Patron, M. (1982). *Practical evaluation.* Thousand Oaks, CA: Sage Publications.

Pedersen, Paul. (1988). *A handbook for developing multicultural awareness.* Alexandria, VA: American Association for Counseling and Development.

Pfeiffer, J. William (Ed.). (1972-1995). *The human resource development annual set.* San Diego, CA: Pfeiffer and Company.

Pfeiffer, J. William, and Arlette C. Ballew. (1988). *Using structured experiences in human resource development.* U.A. Training Technologies 1. San Diego, CA: University Associates, Inc.

Pfeiffer, J. William, and Arlette C. Ballew. (1988). *Using instruments in human resource development.* U.A. Training Technologies 2. San Diego, CA: University Associates, Inc.

Pfeiffer, J. William, and Arlette C. Ballew. (1988). *Using lecturettes, theory, and models in human resource development.* U.A. Training Technologies 3. San Diego, CA: University Associates, Inc.

Pfeiffer, J. William, and Arlette C. Ballew. (1988). *Using role plays in human resource development.* U.A. Training Technologies 4 San Diego, CA: University Associates, Inc.

Pfeiffer, J. William, and Arlette C. Ballew. (1988). *Using case studies, simulations, and games in human resource development.* U.A. Training Technologies 5. San Diego, CA: University Associates, Inc.

Pfeiffer, J. William, and Arlette C. Ballew. (1988). *Design skills in human resource development.* U.A. Training Technologies 6. San Diego, CA: University Associates, Inc.

Pfeiffer, J. William, and Arlette C. Ballew. (1988). *Presentation and evaluation skills in human resource development.* U.A. Training Technologies 7. San Diego, CA: University Associates, Inc.

Pfeiffer, J. William, and John E. Jones (Eds.). (1974-1985). *A handbook of structured experiences.* San Diego, CA: Pfeiffer and Company.

Pusch, Margaret. (1979). *Multicultural education: a cross-cultural approach.* Yarmouth, ME: Intercultural Press.

Reynolds, Angus, and Leonard Nadler. (1993). *The global HRD consultant's and practitioner's handbook.* Amherst, MA: HRD Press.

Rhinesmith, Stephen. (1992). *A managers guide to globalization.* Burr Ridge, IL: Irwin Professional Publishing.

Robinson, Russell D. (1994). *An introduction to helping adults learn and change.* (Revised edition). West Bend, WI: Omnibook Company.

Romiszowski, A. (1981). *Designing instructional systems: decision making in course planning and curriculum.* New York, NY: Nichols Publishing.

Rossett, A. (1988). *Training needs assessment.* Englewood Cliffs, NJ: Educational Technology Publications (Prentice-Hall).

Samovar, Larry, and Richard Porter. (1991). *Intercultural communication, a reader.* (6th Edition). Belmont, CA: Wadsworth.

Schwarz, Roger M. (1994). *The skilled facilitator: practical wisdom for developing effective groups.* San Francisco: Jossey-Bass Publishers.

Sikkeema, Mildred, and Agnes Niyekawa. (1987). *Design for cross-cultural learning.* Yarmouth, ME: Intercultural Press.

Silberman, M. L. (1990). *Active training.* New York, NY: Lexington Books.

Silberman, M. L., J. S. Allender, and J. M. Yanoll. (1972). *The psychology of open teaching and learning.* Boston: Little Brown.

Sredl, Henry, and William Rothwell. (1987). *The ASTD reference guide to professional training and development roles and competencies.* Amherst, MA: Human Resource Development Press.

Smith, Barry J., and Brian L. Delahaye. (1983). *How to be an effective trainer.* New York, NY: John Wiley.

Storti, Craig. (1990). *The art of crossing cultures.* Yarmouth, ME: Intercultural Press.

Storti, Craig. (1994). *Cross-cultural dialogue: 74 brief encounters with cultural diference.* Yarmouth, ME: Intercultural Press.

Stufflebeam, D. L., and A. J. Shinkfield. (1985). *Systematic evaluation.* Boston: Kluwer-Nijhoff.

Swierczek, Frederic. (1988). Culture and training: how do they play away from home? *Training and Development Journal,* Vol. 42, 11. November 1988.

Thiederman, Sondra. (1991). *Bridging cultural barriers for corporate success: how to manage the multicultural work force.* New York, NY: Lexington Books.

Tracy, William A. (Ed.). (1994). *Human resources management and development handbook.* New York, NY: American Management Association.

Tough, Allen. (1967). *Learning without a teacher.* Toronto: Ontario Institute for Studies in Education.

Tough, Allen. (1979). *The adult's learning projects.* Toronto: Ontario Institute for Studies in Education.

Trompenaars, Fons. (1994). *Riding the waves of culture.* Burr Ridge, IL: Irwin Professional Publishing.

Weeks, William, Paul Pedersen, and Richard Brislin. (1985). *A manual of structured experiences for cross-cultural learning.* Yarmouth, ME: Intercultural Press.

Wigglesworth, David C. (1989). *Bibliography of international/intercultural literature.* Alexandria, VA: American Society for Training and Development.

Wigglesworth, David C. (1993). *Resources for workforce diversity.* Fredonia, NY: H.R. Press.

Bibliographer David C. Wigglesworth, Ph. D., is an intercultural/international human resource, management and organization development consultant and president of D.C.W. Research Associates International, P.O. Box 4400, Foster City, CA 94404-0400, Tel.: (415) 573-1864, Fax: (415) 349-7330, Email: dcwigg@aol.com

INDEX

W

Y

V

Adult Learning Systems, Inc. (ALS), is a new organization formed specifically to address issues dealing with intercultural effectiveness. *Adult Education, Human Resource Development* and *Intercultural Communications* address behavioral issues. ALS is specifically concerned with behavioral issues in these fields and how to most effectively make a significant contribution to the field of intercultural service. In the near future, ALS anticipates being able to offer a credit card service.

Forthcoming titles address the topics of **self-directedness through interdependence, facilitation of intercultural work, teamwork,** and an anticipated *four volume collection of poems* by Kenneth L. Pike, representing a scholar's approach to the affective side of life.

An order blank is included below for your convenience. You might just photocopy the form in order not to cut the page from the book.

Name _____

Title _____

Address _____

City _____ State _____ Zip _____

Email address _____

Telephone _____ Fax _____

Adult Learning Systems, Inc.
P.O. Box 458
Duncanville, TX 75138-0458

Training Know-How for Cross-Cultural and Diversity Trainers
$29.95 plus $3.00 S/H. $ _____

Value Option Cards
$29.95 plus $3.00 S/H. $ _____

Texas residents, please add applicable sales tax. $ _____

Total $ _____